Impulse-Control Disorders

THE STATE OF
MENTAL ILLNESS
AND ITS THERAPY

THE STATE OF MENTAL ILLNESS AND ITS THERAPY

Impulse-Control Disorders

Autumn Libal

Mason Crest

Mason Crest
450 Parkway Drive, Suite D
Broomall, PA 19008
www.masoncrest.com

Printed in the Hashemite Kingdom of Jordan.

First printing
9 8 7 6 5 4 3 2 1

Series ISBN: 978-1-4222-2819-7
ISBN: 978-1-4222-2827-2
ebook ISBN: 978-1-4222-8988-4

The Library of Congress has cataloged the
    hardcopy format(s) as follows:

        Library of Congress Cataloging-in-Publication Data

Libal, Autumn.
  [Drug therapy and impulse control disorders]
  Impulse-control disorders / Autumn Libal.
      pages cm. – (The state of mental illness and its therapy)
  Audience: Age 12.
  Audience: Grade 7 to 8.
  Revision of: Drug therapy and impulse control disorders. 2004.
  Includes bibliographical references and index.
  ISBN 978-1-4222-2827-2 (hardcover) – ISBN 978-1-4222-2819-7 (series) – ISBN 978-1-4222-8988-4
(ebook)
  1. Impulse control disorders–Juvenile literature. 2. Impulse control disorders–Chemotherapy–Ju-
venile literature. I. Title.
  RC569.5.I46L53 2014
  616.85'84061–dc23
                            2013008198

Produced by Vestal Creative Services.

www.vestalcreative.com

This book is meant to educate and should not be used as an alternative to appropriate medical care. Its cre-
ators have made every effort to ensure that the information presented is accurate—but it is not intended to
substitute for the help and services of trained professionals.

Picture Credits:
Artville: pp. 32, 45, 68, 75, 76, 78, 79, 80, 81, 97, 102, 105, 112, 118. Autumn Libal: pp. 13, 14, 19, 21, 24, 37,
55, 63, 64, 70, 73, 91, 95, 98, 116. Benjamin Stewart: pp. 60. 122. Comstock: pp. 35, 40, 49, 65, 66, 82, 86, 100,
104. Corbis: pp. 114, 121, 123. National Library of Medicine: p. 42. Photo Alto: p. 33. Photo Disc: pp. 36, 39,
46, 52, 54, 74, 84, 88, 107, 108. Rubberball: pp. 10, 30, 47, 92. Stockbyte: pp. 94, 110. The individuals in these
images are models, and the images are for illustrative purposes only. To the best knowledge of the publisher, all
other images are in the public domain. If any image has been inadvertently uncredited or miscredited, please
notify Vestal Creative Services, Vestal, New York 13850, so that rectification can be made for future printings.

CONTENTS

Introduction
by Mary Ann McDonnell

T eenagers have reason to be interested in psychiatric disorders and their treatment. Friends, family members, and even teens themselves may experience one of these disorders. Using scenarios adolescents will understand, this series explains various psychiatric disorders and the drugs that treat them.

Diagnosis and treatment of psychiatric disorders in children between six and eighteen years old are well studied and documented in the scientific journals. A paper appearing in the *Journal of the American Academy of Child and Adolescent Psychiatry* in 2010 estimated that 49.5 percent of all adolescents aged 13 to 18 were affected by at least one psychiatric disorder. Various other studies have reported similar findings. Needless to say, many children and adolescents are suffering from psychiatric disorders and are in need of treatment.

Many children have more than one psychiatric disorder, which complicates their diagnoses and treatment plans. Psychiatric disorders often occur together. For instance, a person with a sleep disorder may also be depressed; a teenager with attention-deficit/hyperactivity disorder (ADHD) may also have a substance-use disorder. In psychiatry, we call this comorbidity. Much research addressing this issue has led to improved diagnosis and treatment.

The most common child and adolescent psychiatric disorders are:anxiety disorders, depressive disorders, and ADHD. Sleep disorders, sexual disorders, eating disorders, substance-abuse disorders, and psychotic disorders are also quite common. This series has volumes that address each of these disorders.

Major depressive disorders have been the most commonly diagnosed mood disorders for children and adolescents. Researchers don't agree as to how common mania and bipolar disorder are in children. Some experts believe that manic episodes in children and adolescents are underdiagnosed. Many times, a mood disturbance may co-occur with another psychiatric disorder. For instance, children with ADHD may also be depressed. ADHD is just one psychiatric disorder that is a major health concern for children, adolescents, and adults. Studies of ADHD have reported prevalence rates among children that range from two to 12 percent.

Failure to understand or seek treatment for psychiatric disorders put children and young adults at risk of developing substance-use disorders. For example, recent research indicates that those with ADHD who were treated with medication were 85 percent less likely to develop a substance-use disorder. Results like these emphasize the importance of timely diagnosis and treatment.

Early diagnosis and treatment may prevent these children from developing further psychological problems. Books like those in this series provide important information, a vital first step toward increased awareness of psychological disorders; knowledge and understanding can shed light on even the most difficult subject. These books should never, however, be viewed as a substitute for professional consultation. Psychiatric testing and an evaluation by a licensed professional are recommended to determine the needs of the child or adolescent and to establish an appropriate treatment plan.

Foreword
by Donald Esherick

We live in a society filled with technology—from computers surfing the Internet to automobiles operating on gas and batteries. In the midst of this advanced society, diseases, illnesses, and medical conditions are treated and often cured with the administration of drugs, many of which were unknown thirty years ago. In the United States, we are fortunate to have an agency, the Food and Drug Administration (FDA), which monitors the development of new drugs and then determines whether the new drugs are safe and effective for use in human beings.

When a new drug is developed, a pharmaceutical company usually intends that drug to treat a single disease or family of diseases. The FDA reviews the company's research to determine if the drug is safe for use in the population at large and if it effectively treats the targeted illnesses. When the FDA finds that the drug is safe and effective, it approves the drug for treating that specific disease or condition. This is called the labeled indication.

During the routine use of the drug, the pharmaceutical company and physicians often observe that a drug treats other medical conditions besides what is indicated in the labeling. While the labeling will not include the treatment of the particular condition, a physician can still prescribe the drug to a patient with this disease. This is known as an unlabeled or off-label indication. This series contains information about both the labeled and off-label indications of psychiatric drugs.

I have reviewed the books in this series from the perspective of the pharmaceutical industry and the FDA, specifically focusing on the labeled indications, uses, and known side effects of these drugs. Further information can be found on the FDA's website (www.FDA.gov).

A person with an impulse control disorder may have difficulty controlling his anger.

Chapter One

What Are Impulse Control Disorders?

The throbbing in his hand snapped Jerry back to reality. He looked down. Warm blood dripped from his knuckles. Jagged pieces of glass glinted from the windowsill and floor. He watched the cuts in his pale skin yawn open as he flexed his fingers. They would need stitches.

"Hey, what's wrong with you, man?"

He turned. His two friends stood next to the overturned table. Frightened, they backed away from Jerry. Ice from their spilled drinks crunched beneath their feet. The playing cards from their upset poker game were scattered in a sea of black spades and red hearts. Jerry looked at the clock, and his already racing heart began to pound. He dove to his hands and knees and desperately scooped up the cards. "Oh no! My dad's gonna be home any minute. Help me clean this up before he gets here."

His friends looked at each other. "No way, man. I think it's time for us to go." They nodded to each other and reached for the door.

"Please, guys," Jerry pleaded. "He's gonna kill me when he sees this."

"Look, Jerry." His friend spat the words. "I don't know what's wrong with you, but you said you wanted to play cards. We didn't know you were gonna put your fist through a window."

"Yeah," his other friend agreed. "If we'd known you were such a sore loser, we would have just let you win." They stepped outside, letting the door slam behind them.

Jerry looked at the chaos scattered around him. It was like a tornado had gone through . . . a tornado named "Jerry." He grabbed a dishtowel and wrapped it around his aching hand. Leaning back against the kitchen cabinets, he put his toweled hand over his eyes. He gulped back the lump forming in his throat and tried to squeeze the tears back behind his eyelids. He felt terrible about the window, but he felt even worse that he'd frightened his friends. What was the big deal anyway? He'd just lost a poker game. He couldn't believe he'd gotten so angry over something so stupid. Why couldn't he just control himself like other people?

Discussion

An impulse is an urge or desire that comes on suddenly without prior consideration. People feel both emotional and physical impulses. For example, when having a great time with your best friend, you might feel a sudden impulse to give her a hug. When watching your favorite soccer team score a goal, you might jump up and cheer. If you see somebody else get sick, you might feel unexpectedly nauseous yourself. Waking up from a bad dream, you could feel an abrupt and undeniable need to switch on a light. These are all examples of common emotional impulses.

In addition to the impulses that you are aware of, you are also experiencing unconscious physical impulses all the time. Your brain constantly sends messages causing you to breathe, blink, move your hands, walk, and perform all the other functions of your body. These impulses are necessary for your survival, but you don't have to think about them in order to make them happen.

However, there are many impulses that you do think about, to which you make conscious responses. You feel the impulse to go to the bathroom, but then you must control the impulse until you are able to get to a restroom. You could get angry with your teacher and feel an impulse to yell at him, but you stop yourself because you know that yelling will get you into trouble. Sometimes you may find it easier to control an impulse than at other times. Every once in a while, you may even lose control of an impulse that you know you should have resisted. This happens to everyone to a certain degree and is a normal part of life. Some people, however, lose so much control over certain impulses that they develop an impulse control disorder.

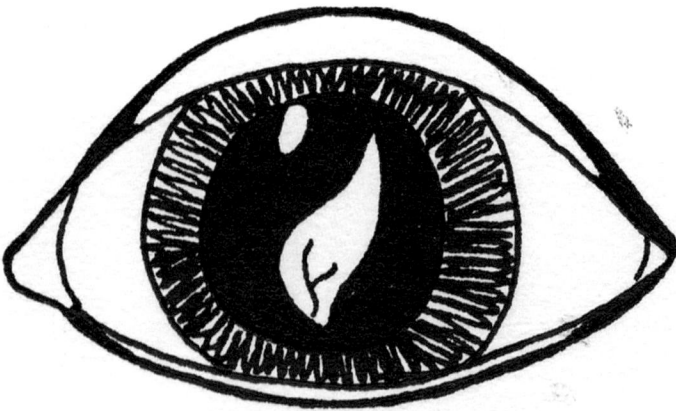

Those people who have a compulsion to set fires may have an impulse control disorder called pyromania.

When people have impulse control disorders, the impulses they would normally be able to control become so strong that they may seem irresistible. In the book *Handbook of Childhood Impulse Disorders and ADHD: Theory and Practice*, Leonard F. Koziol uses the example of a "tic" to explain what these types of impulses are like. A tic is an involuntary movement in a part of the body that a person would normally be able to control. For example, one's eyelid may spasm uncontrollably or the muscles at the corner of a person's mouth may periodically contract, pulling the person's lips into a grimace. Koziol explains that the behavioral impulses associated with impulse control disorders can be thought of as the result of a mental tic. The person can lose so much conscious control over the impulsive action that she may not even realize what she is doing until after she has done it.

Losing control over an impulse, even a very serious one, does not automatically mean that you have an impulse control disorder. When Jerry loses the poker game, he is unable to control his anger. He overturns the table and punches a window, hurting himself and scaring his friends. Such a violent over-reaction could be part of a larger impulse control disorder. But it could also be a sign of something else that is going on in Jerry's life. Sometimes people lose control because they are experiencing extreme amounts of stress, have an illness that is affecting their ability to think clearly, are under the influence of drugs or alcohol, or are facing some other factor that is temporarily influencing their ability to maintain control.

criteria: Tests or requirements that must be met for making a decision.

There are a number of different types of impulse control disorders. Each one has a specific set of criteria to help doctors determine if the patient has an impulse control disorder or if his behavior is caused by some other circumstance in his life.

chronic: Continuing for a long period of time.

intermittent: Starting and stopping or alternating.

Many psychiatric disorders involve a loss of impulse control. Eating disorders, obsessive-compulsive disorder, attention-deficit/hyperactivity disorder, and substance abuse are all characterized by an inability to control certain impulses. However, each of these has its own category and designation in the *Diagnostic and Statistical Manual of Mental Disorders*, fourth edition, text revision (called the DSM-IV-TR).

In addition to these disorders, the medical field recognizes five specific impulse control disorders that exist independently of these other overarching categories. They are intermittent explosive disorder, kleptomania, pyromania, pathological gambling, and trichotillomania. Over time, enough people have been identified with common symptoms to give each of these five disorders its own name and category. However, some people experience chronic difficulties in controlling impulses that are not part of these five specific disorders or any other category of mental disorder but that are still serious enough to be considered disorders. For these people, there is another category called impulse control disorder not otherwise specified.

Intermittent Explosive Disorder

A person with intermittent explosive disorder performs acts very much like the ones Jerry committed. The person has aggressive impulses that he cannot resist and that cause him to destroy property or hurt others.

Many people overreact when they are angry, but they do not have intermittent explosive disorder. It is quite common for people to express extreme anger through actions such as slamming a fist on a table or yelling, but a person with intermittent explosive disorder acts out far more violently, destroying objects of value and threatening to harm or actually harming others. Furthermore, the person's actions are completely out of proportion with the situation. For example, someone might be justifiably angry to find that her car has a flat tire and might even kick the vehicle. The person with intermittent explosive disorder, however, would experience anger that is inappropriate for the situation. Perhaps she would begin screaming at other people in the car, putting dents in the vehicle, and threatening to drive the car over a cliff.

There are many things that can cause someone to overreact when she is angry. For example, people with psychiatric conditions like borderline personality disorder or bipolar disorder may have inappropriate reactions to certain situations. In order to be diagnosed with intermittent explosive disorder, the person's actions must not be caused by any other disorders, substance abuse, or extenuating circumstances.

In the above story, Jerry experiences an explosive outburst that is grossly out of proportion with how a person would reasonably react to losing a card game. Sometimes people experience a terrible explosive episode only once, but if Jerry has uncontrollable impulses like this one periodically, he may be suffering from intermittent explosive disorder. To know for sure, however, he would have to seek a medical opinion.

Whereas aggressive and violent acts are increasingly common in our society, medically diagnosable intermittent explosive disorder seems to be rare. It occurs in men more often than in women. There

borderline personality disorder: A personality disorder characterized by difficulty in maintaining interpersonal relationships, instability of self-image, expressions of appropriate feelings, and control over impulses.

bipolar disorder: A psychological condition characterized by periods of extreme highs and extreme lows.

extenuating: Additional circumstances that may give partial justification for an act.

is a lack of reliable research into the causes, onset, and course of intermittent explosive disorder, but the information that is available suggests that people develop the disorder between childhood and their early twenties. Furthermore, different people experience the disorder in very different ways. When it comes to treatment, some people respond very well to psychiatric therapy, while other people find medication helpful, while still other people receive very little relief from either of these forms of medical intervention.

hallucinations: Sensory perceptions without evidence of their existence.

conclusive: Gives proof, resolves all doubts or disbelief.

Kleptomania

Kleptomania is an impulse control disorder in which a person repeatedly steals. If a person repeatedly steals objects because he needs or wants them but cannot afford them, however, the person does not have kleptomania. People with kleptomania steal things they do not need and that have very little monetary value. They often throw away the objects or give them away as gifts soon after stealing them. The person with kleptomania feels a growing sense of tension or internal chaos before stealing. Directly after stealing, the person feels a sense of relief, as though the tension has broken. In order for a diagnosis of kleptomania to be given, a doctor must determine that the stealing is not caused by another condition (like hallucinations or a personality disorder), is not done to express anger or vengeance, and is not caused by the influence of drugs or alcohol.

People with kleptomania know that stealing is wrong and that their behavior would seem irrational or even absurd to others. Knowing that their behavior is wrong and illegal, but feeling unable to control themselves, leads many people with kleptomania to feel depressed, guilty, and fearful of being caught. Unlike people who steal because they want to or because they cannot afford something

People with kleptomania may steal very small, inexpensive items. They may even steal items they don't really want.

that they need, people with kleptomania usually do not plan to steal ahead of time. Instead, they steal when the impulse urges them to do so without prior thought to what they will steal or what the consequences will be. Although many people with kleptomania don't keep the stolen objects, some people will stash the objects away or try to secretly return them to the place from which they were stolen.

Although there is a lack of conclusive data on the subject, it appears that kleptomania can develop at any time between childhood and adulthood, but that it is rare for it to develop in late adulthood. Kleptomania appears to affect women more often than men.

Pyromania

Pyromania is an impulse control disorder in which a person purposefully sets fires. As in kleptomania, a person with pyromania feels a building sense of tension or unrest directly before setting a fire and feels relief or pleasure from setting the fire and observing the fire and its effects. Usually, the person is fascinated not only by fire but by other things having to do with fire, such as lighters, fire alarms, and fire departments. People with pyromania are so fascinated by fire and things associated with fire that they often even become fire fighters so that they can be close to fire.

People with pyromania do not set fires out of anger, for financial reasons (such as being awarded insurance money for lost property), or to destroy evidence of other crimes. When considering a diagnosis of pyromania, a doctor must also be careful to determine that the fire-setting activities are not caused by other mental disorders (like schizophrenia or **conduct disorder**) and that the person was not acting with judgment impaired by **delusions**, hallucinations, alcohol, or substance abuse.

Unlike kleptomania in which people do not plan ahead to steal, people with pyromania often do plan on starting a fire prior to carrying out the act. However, in this planning stage they may not consider the consequences, such as property destruction and harm to themselves or others. However, some people with pyromania feel **gratification** from the damage their fires cause.

Although fire-setting in children and adolescents is rather common, true pyromania is a rare disorder and occurs in males more often than in females. Most of the fire-setting done by young people is due not to an impulse control disorder but to other external social influences or adjustment-related disorders. For example, young people may set fires because of peer pressure, as part of erratic behavior associated with attention-deficit/hyperactiv-

conduct disorder: A behavioral disorder in childhood characterized by persistent violation of others' rights and age-appropriate social norms and values.

delusions: An incorrect belief based on a misinterpretation of reality and that persists despite evidence that it is false.

gratification: The state of feeling a sense of pleasure.

constructively: Describing an action that causes improvement or positive effects.

There seem to be three ways in which kleptomania is experienced:

- Sporadic. A person with sporadic kleptomania has short periods of stealing separated by long periods of time in which she does not steal. The person, for example, may steal many things over the course of three days and then not steal anything for a year.
- Episodic. In episodic kleptomania, the periods of stealing are longer and separated by periods of not stealing. A person with episodic kleptomania may regularly steal objects for three months and then stop stealing for five months.
- Chronic. A person with chronic kleptomania steals on a regular basis. There may be periods of time when she steals more and periods of time when she steals less, but the stealing remains a habitual part of her life.

ity disorder, or because of frustrating circumstances that they do not know how to deal with constructively. It is also relatively common for young people to set fires simply by accident when experimenting with things like matches and lighters. An isolated incident of experimenting with fire or purposeful fire-setting is not a sign of pyromania.

Pathological Gambling

Pathological gambling is a disorder in which a person gambles to such an excessive and uncontrolled extent that it disrupts his social, familial, and working relationships and functioning. Many people gamble, and many of these people may even gamble to excess but do not have a pathological gambling disor-

pathological: Something that is caused by a disease or repetitive, compulsive behavior that is so abnormally severe as to be characteristic of illness or disease.

"Communicative arson" is a term given to situations in which someone has purposefully set a fire in an attempt to communicate some need or desire to others. Communicative arson usually happens among people with mental disabilities or people who are dependent on others for their care and well-being. For example, a child in the foster care system is dependent on social workers and other state employees to advocate for her needs. In one case, a child felt unsafe in her current foster home and repeatedly requested a transfer to a new home. When her request for a transfer was ignored, she set fire to her bedroom in her foster home. She did this to both express her anger and frustration and because she thought that if she burned her bedroom, her social worker would be forced to move her into a different home. This fire-setting is an example of communicative arson and even though the fire was purposefully set, it is not related to pyromania.

der. According to the DSM-IV-TR, to be diagnosed with pathological gambling disorder, a person must have five or more of the following characteristics:

1. The person is often absorbed in thinking about gambling, devising ways to get money to gamble with, strategizing for his next gambling venture, or reliving former gambling episodes.
2. The person needs to risk more money each time he gambles in order to feel the same excitement that he previously felt with less money.
3. The person has tried on a number of occasions to stop or reduce his gambling but fails.
4. Attempting to cut back has a negative affect on the person's mood making him tense, peevish, or unpredictable.
5. The person uses gambling to escape from other stressful circumstances or emotional problems in his life. For example,

the person might gamble to escape from thinking about problems at work, difficulties with his family, or to alleviate depression.

6. The person participates in a behavior known as "chasing one's losses" in which the person, after losing money gambling one day, returns the next day or soon after to try to win back the money.

7. The person lies about his gambling to try to keep others from knowing the extent of his behavior. Not only does the person lie to family and friends about his gambling he might even lie to mental health professionals at the very same time that he is seeking treatment for his gambling.

peevish: argumentative, easily angered, moody, or ill tempered.

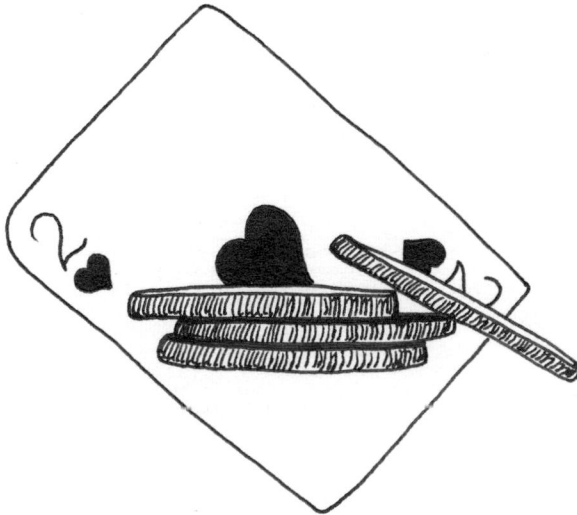

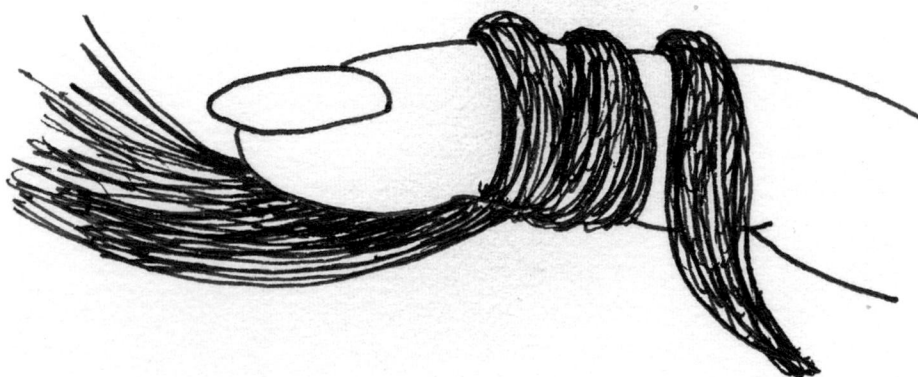

A person with trichotillomania feels a compulsion to pull out her own hair. She may do so to the point that she has bald spots on her head.

8. The person has engaged in criminal activity, like theft or fraud, to get money with which to gamble.
9. The person's excessive gambling has caused him to risk or lose jobs, relationships, or other important positive aspects of his life.
10. The person's excessive gambling has led to debt or financial instability so serious that he needs to turn to other people for money or support.

Once it has been determined that a person's gambling behaviors meet five or more of these criteria, a doctor must also determine that the person's gambling is not part of a manic episode. People experiencing mania may engage in binge behaviors like excessive eating, drinking, gambling, exorbitant spending, extreme amounts of exercise, or other types of unrestrained activity. If a person's impulsive gambling is part of a manic episode, then the person does not have pathological gambling disorder.

The growing sense of internal tension that many people with impulse control disorders feel before they engage in impulsive behaviors is not necessarily related to stressful external circumstances. For example, one person with trichotillomania might feel the need to pull hair during a stressful situation like a math test. However, another person with trichotillomania might feel the impulse during periods of "engaged relaxation" (when the body is relaxed but the mind is occupied by other things) like watching a movie or daydreaming about an upcoming party.

Trichotillomania

Trichotillomania, also called TTM or trich for short, is an impulse control disorder in which a person habitually pulls out her own hair, causing significant hair loss. As with other impulse control disorders, a sense of tension or internal disruption precedes the impulse to pull hair, and this tension is relieved once the impulse to pull the hair has been satisfied.

When considering a diagnosis of trichotillomania, a doctor must determine that the individual's hair loss is not caused by another medical condition like a serious rash, infection of the skin and hair follicles, or genetic hair loss. Many children go through short phases of behaviors like nail biting and hair pulling, so a doctor must also determine that the hair pulling is more than a

manic: Describes a state of abnormally intense activity that may be accompanied by extreme personality changes, violence, quickly alternating moods, or a dramatic sense of happiness.

binge: Unrestrained or self-indulgent activities.

Sorting Through the Symptoms

Many psychiatric disorders' symptoms overlap or appear very similar. It is important to see an experienced practitioner who can disentangle the symptoms related to impulse control, mood disorders, attention-deficit disorder, and anxiety. Finding a practitioner within this area of expertise is essential to proper diagnosis and treatment.

short-term habit and is having a significant impact on other aspects of the person's life. For example, the individual's hair pulling may have caused hair loss that is so noticeable that she is embarrassed to go to school, or long-term problems with hair pulling and hair loss may lead to low self-esteem that keeps the person from participating in social activities.

Individuals with trichotillomania may be preoccupied with hair beyond pulling the hair out. They may closely inspect the pulled hairs, eat the hairs (a behavior known as trichophagia), or even try to secretly pull hair from other people. People with trichotillomania commonly have other habits, like nail-biting and skin-picking, and other disorders, like obsessive-compulsive disorder and eating disorders. If the hair pulling is a direct result of another disorder, like obsessive-compulsive disorder, then the person should not be diagnosed with trichotillomania.

A person with trichotillomania might pull hair from any part of her body, but the most common places from which people pull hair are the head, eyebrows, and eyelashes. A common myth is that hair that is pulled out will not grow back. In very extreme cases of trichotillomania where the condition has existed for a long period of time, long-term damage may be done to the hair follicles, root, and blood supply. In most cases, however, a person's hair will grow back in its entirety once she seeks treatment and stops pulling.

Impulse Control Disorder Not Otherwise Specified

Explosive anger, stealing, fire-setting, gambling, and hair pulling are certainly not the only ways in which people experience impulse control disorders. The category impulse control disorder not otherwise specified is given to patients who repeatedly fail to resist an impulse that is not one of the five impulses discussed above. Just as in the other forms of impulse control disorders, the person's behavior must not be caused by another disorder (like obsessive-compulsive disorder or schizophrenia) and must be severe enough that it significantly impairs the person's regular personal, emotional, social, or occupational functioning. The following story is an example of a person with an impulse control disorder not otherwise specified.

The first time Julia cut herself she thought it was by accident. She had been sitting at her desk with her unfinished artwork spread before her. Dark charcoal smudges blurred the lines of her self-portrait. Scraps of paper littered the table like autumn leaves in a black-and-white photograph. Half-dried glue oozed from the lip of an overturned bottle, and a thin layer of pastel dust coated everything with a strange orange-purple hue.

She looked around her, immobilized by the anarchy of colors and artist materials. Her portfolio for design school was due the next day. How could she give order to the mess and produce a quality piece of work by tomorrow? The chaos of the room was seeping into her head. She couldn't think, couldn't breath, felt too tense to exhale. A thick cloud of mental quicksand was sucking her under. This must be what drowning feels like, she thought as she began to panic. Then something sliced through the fog and captured her attention with a sudden urgency. Julia looked down. She had been holding her artist's knife, poised to cut a clean, sweeping line through a piece of cardboard. Preoccupied with her other thoughts, she must have closed her hand around the blade.

Julia looked at the thin red line drawn across her palm and the droplets oozing from it onto the stark whiteness of her drawing paper. Her head felt suddenly clear. This was it, she thought, looking at the simple crimson dots. This was her self, her very essence dripping onto the paper. She examined how cleanly the knife had cut through her skin—such a thin layer between the chaos on the outside and the pure, purposeful, living inside. Staring at her blood was like an awakening. This was her truest self, her only self, exposed. A sense of calm swept over her. It was like the cut was a dividing line between the confused, uncertain, frantic Julia before and the instantly aware, centered, knowing Julia who was now examining her flayed hand. *So everything comes down to this*, she thought, *flesh and blood and a beating heart*. It was like the static in her mind had come into quiet focus, and she could work again.

She could not say when precisely she began to cut herself purposefully. Over time, however, she began to think of the calm she had experienced at her worktable that day. She kept a razor blade in a little box in the bathroom, and when she felt the low humming beginning in the back of her mind, she would sit and concentrate on staying calm. But sometimes the buzzing would rise to a fevered pitch, and then she would take that razor blade from its little box and draw a thin line across her skin. The buzzing in her head dissipated like a swarm of bees in a sudden gust of wind.

For a moment, watching the liquid red beads peek up through the separated skin made her feel calm, refocused, and completely in the present. But then guilt would wash over her. She would wrap the blade in tissue paper and secret it back into the little box. Dabbing at her skin with rubbing alcohol, she would vow never to cut herself again. Inevitably, however, when the tension began to rise in her another day, she would return to the box with its blade inside.

Discussion

Self-cutting and self-mutilation are little understood and yet surprisingly common. There is much debate in the field of psychiatry over why people cut or hurt themselves. It was once thought that any form of self-harm must be an expression of hidden suicidal tendencies. In recent years, however, a growing amount of autobiographical material and academic study of the matter has suggested that self-cutting is an impulse that has nothing to do with suicide.

In the above story, Julia cuts herself on impulse to relieve a growing internal tension. Furthermore, she has not done this only once but continues to give in to the impulse despite attempts to stop. Her behavior has signs of an impulse control disorder, but self-cutting is not one of the five specifically classified impulse control disorders discussed above. Therefore, a psychiatrist or medical practitioner, if determining that Julia's actions are not caused by depression, suicidal tendencies, or other physical or psychological disorders, might diagnose Julia's condition as an impulse control disorder not otherwise specified.

A person with an impulse disorder may struggle with depression as she attempts to hide her psychiatric difficulties from the rest of the world.

Chapter Two

History of Treatment and Drug Therapy

ary grew up in a very strict, Catholic home. The family attended church every Sunday, and her parents sent her to Catholic school. Her mother made Mary sing in the church choir and volunteer at every church picnic and fund-raiser. Every night after dinner the children sat around the dinner table with their heads bowed while their father read from the family Bible.

Throughout her teenage years, Mary struggled emotionally. To all outward appearances, she was like any other teenage girl. Even Mary's parents never realized anything was wrong. But Mary felt like she was suffocating under a terrible secret. Being around others made her restless. When she was in public spaces, she felt as if the buildings, people, cars, and movement were crushing her, closing in from all sides like one of those shrinking rooms in a bad horror film.

In stores, the rows upon rows of cluttered objects made her brain spin, her breath catch in her throat, and her hands vibrate down into the tips of her fingers.

At first, Mary tried dealing with these feelings of inner panic by arranging and rearranging things around her. When she was in a store, she would shift items around on the shelves, trying to make sense of the clutter and force it into order. But then she began taking things off the shelves and putting them into her pockets. She didn't want to steal, and she had no use for the things she was taking, but somehow taking them made her feel better, like she was taking control. When she carried objects out of a store, she felt a great sense of relief, like some dam in her mind had broken, allowing the waters to flow freely again.

Not all thieves are greedy "bad guys." Some struggle with a very real psychiatric disorder that causes their behavior.

Kleptomania may create feelings of shame, fear, and despair.

Afraid that people would find out her shameful secret stealing, Mary became more and more isolated. She had never felt particularly religious herself, and as she got older, she grew away from the church. When Mary graduated from high school, she saw college as an excuse to get away from her family and town. She felt optimistic about starting her life anew. She moved away from home, vowed to stop stealing, and put all of her energy into beginning a redeemed life. As the pressure of her classes grew, however, Mary's need to steal grew too. She felt herself slipping down the same path of isolation, fear, and impulsiveness.

One day, Mary's situation grew suddenly worse when she was called into the dean of the school's office. A security tape had caught Mary shoplifting in the school's bookstore. The dean explained that behavior such as this would not be tolerated and that without reform, Mary would find herself in danger of being asked to leave the school. Mary felt panic burn through her body and mind. She wanted to change, needed to change, yet no matter how hard she tried she just kept on the same self-destructive path.

That night, alone in her dorm room, Mary thought about how much comfort her mother and father received from going to church. They were such good people. They never raised their voices, hurt others, or broke laws. Maybe they had the key to what would cure her of her terrible ways, she thought. With this in mind, Mary joined the Catholic church in her college town.

Once she joined the church, however, Mary began to feel even worse. The priest told the congregation that God loved them. But how could God love her, Mary wondered, when she couldn't stop stealing? Mary feared that no one would love her if they knew the truth about her. She began to feel like an impostor as she sat in her pew among the devout women praying their rosaries and pious men singing heartfelt hymns.

On Sundays, Mary went to confession to tell the priest what she'd done and ask for forgiveness of her sins; however, she always glossed over her "sin" and never told the priest exactly what it was she was doing. Each week she vowed to change her ways. She left church feeling cleansed and determined to live a good life. A few days later, however, she would find herself once again leaving a store with cheap merchandise in her pockets. Finally, Mary went to see her priest and broke down. She confided in him, telling him of her guilt and shame. She said that she loved God and tried to be good, but no matter how hard she tried, she failed. She thought there must be something bad, even evil, in her.

Mary's priest assured her that she wasn't bad or evil, but definitely needed to find help for her condition. After she described her actions to him, he asked if she'd ever sought a medical opinion. He explained that sometimes our behavior isn't just about what we intentionally want to do. He said that some mental conditions and physical disorders affect our behavior. He said that she was right to turn to her faith for help but that medicine might be able to help her too.

Religion can be a source of guilt and shame for those who suffer from psychiatric disorders—but it can also offer comfort and strength.

When Mary took her priest's advice and sought medical attention, she was diagnosed with the impulse control disorder kleptomania. She was shocked to know that she had a psychiatric condition, but at the same time she was incredibly relieved to learn that she wasn't simply a "bad" or "evil" person. When she described the feelings of panic, isolation, and guilt that drove her need to steal, her psychiatrist prescribed a medication known as an SSRI that he thought might ease these impulses. When he prescribed the medication to Mary, he was very careful to explain that a psychiatric drug such as this one could not be a sudden cure. The medicine would have to be used in combination with other forms of therapy and behavior modification. He also told Mary that by joining a church, she had actually already made big strides on her journey to wellness. He explained that being part of a supportive community was an important aspect of treatment and that many people found religion to be the perfect place for solace and strength. Now that she had a word and a treatment for her condition, Mary was able to return to her church with a new sense of optimism and inner peace.

Talking with someone older or with a counselor or religious person can help troubled youth find their way toward healing.

Although Mary initially experienced increased feelings of failure after attending church, eventually she found that church could play a role on her road to recovery.

Discussion

Historically, impulse control disorders have been difficult to diagnose and to treat. Some people even claim that these disorders don't exist at all, that they are just excuses people use to justify improper behavior. This of course is not true. But there are many reasons, some simple and some complicated, why people in our society find conditions like impulse control disorders difficult to understand.

In the above story, we see that religion has a major influence on how Mary experiences her impulse control disorder. When Mary reenters the church, she does not immediately find the comfort she is looking for. That is because her kleptomania causes her to commit acts that are the opposite of how she believes a "good" and "moral" person would behave.

Both in social and religious communities, if a person is suffering from an impulse control disorder, she and others may see her

Throughout human history, religion has been one of the biggest influences on the development of societies, cultures, and belief systems. North American society is often called a "secular" society; in other words, it is not based on religion. For example, unlike many other countries in the world, the governments of the United States of America and Canada are run by political parties rather than by religious bodies. Calling our society secular, however, gives an inaccurate picture of how much religion has and continues to influence us. As with all societies, religion has had a strong influence on North American society and beliefs. The values of Western religions like Judaism, Protestantism, Catholicism, and Islam influence everything from the way we treat each other to the way we run our governments. Many people in our society are raised within a specific religious belief system, and this belief system will influence how they interpret the events and world around them. Many other people, even if not raised within a religion, turn to religion in times of need, such as when diagnosed with a serious illness.

actions as a lack of belief or as immorality rather than as a medical condition. This is what happens in the above story. Mary cannot reconcile her behavior with the beliefs of her religion. She goes to her church for comfort, but then feels even guiltier when she relapses into impulsive actions. The more she compares her own actions with her religion's values and ideals, the more despair and self-loathing she feels. She thinks that if she is religious enough and puts enough faith in God, she should be able to stop herself from stealing. Mary is very lucky, however, that the priest from her church suggests she might be suffering from a medical condition. Once Mary seeks medical council and realizes she is suffering from a legitimate medical condition, she is able to find comfort and emotional support in her religious community.

Even though we may not always be aware of religion's influence, it plays a very real role in how our society thinks about right and wrong.

Religions are certainly not the only way that social values develop. Common attitudes toward impulse control disorders are influenced by other factors as well. For a long time, Western medicine and society have believed in a separation of mind and body. With the view that the mind and body are separate came the belief that behavior, unlike many other aspects of the human body, is conscious, intentional, and controllable. Beliefs such as these cause some people with impulse control disorders and their families to deny the existence of their condition.

Our cultural values emphasize the strength of the individual and personal character and promote the ideal that our actions are a result of exercising willpower and conscious decision making. Our society rewards characteristics like "independence," "strength," and "self-sufficiency." In school, we learn things like "where there's a will, there's a way," and "you can do anything if you just put your mind to it." In many respects, these are good lessons, but sometimes people believe so strongly in the power of the individual that they forget that there are some struggles that people cannot conquer on their own. Many people believe that all individuals can behave "properly" if they simply want to badly enough. If a person acts improperly or commits a crime, people believe that the action reveals a flaw in her character rather than a legitimate medical condition. For example, many people would say that a person who steals could stop if she really wanted and that her continued stealing is not an illness but a sign that she is "bad" or "weak." However, in Mary's story we see that Mary sincerely wants to stop stealing, but even with her strong desire she cannot change her behavior.

In the past, there was no treatment for people with impulse control disorders because such people were assumed to be "common"

Western: Something that is based on Greco-Roman traditions, or pertaining to the countries of Europe and America.

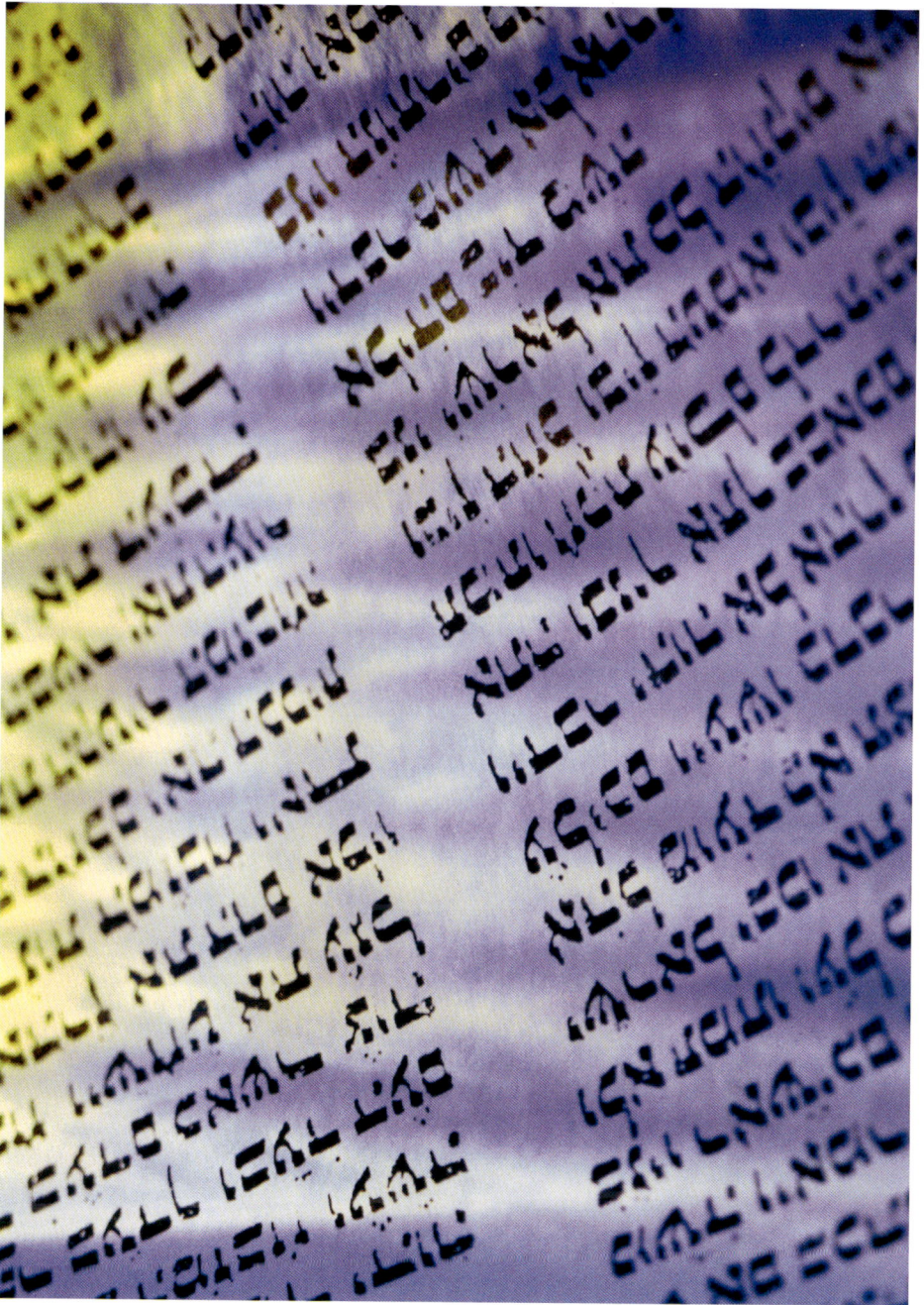

The Judaic scripture has influenced the cultural values of
North America.

A hundred years ago, someone with a psychiatric disorder would have been separated from the rest of society, just as criminals were; she might also be restrained in a straight jacket, as this woman was.

criminals. In our society, people who harm others, steal, or set fires are usually "treated" by being put in jail or receiving other legally determined punishments. Today, it is still all too common that people with impulse control disorders are turned over to the criminal justice system instead of receiving medical treatment.

The problem of separating people with mental disorders from criminals is magnified by the fact that criminals sometimes claim to have impulse control disorders in the hopes of lessening their punishments or getting away with their crimes. For example, an abusive parent might claim to have intermittent explosive disorder to justify hurting his child, even though he does not have the disorder. When caught stealing, a robber might claim to have kleptomania, even though she does not. False claims like these lead to suspicion and doubt when people who really do have impulse control disorders need help.

Many other cultural and social values encourage people to doubt the existence of conditions such as impulse control disorders. For example, impulse control disorders have many of the same characteristics as addictions. In most addictions, people are dependent on a substance. In impulse control disorders, people are "addicted" to a behavior. The person "needs" to gamble, steal, or pull hair to function, the same way a smoker might "need" a cigarette to get through her day. Although many people are now realizing the benefits of medication in helping break substance addictions, for a long time people believed that the only way to overcome addiction was to quit "cold turkey."

Groups like Alcoholics Anonymous and others promote the idea that changing our behavior is a matter of willpower and depends on a person's ability to recognize her weaknesses and claim responsibility for her actions. Groups such as these have helped thousands of people and families through the struggles of addiction. They have also, however, played a large part in creating and promoting the idea that individuals can modify their behavior if they simply want to badly enough and that failure to modify behavior shows a weakness of character or desire. Beliefs such as these are, of course, not

Brand Names vs. Generic Names

Talking about psychiatric drugs can be confusing, because every drug has at least two names: its "generic name" and the "brand name" that the pharmaceutical company uses to market the drug. Generic names come from the drugs' chemical structures, while brand names are used by drug companies to inspire consumers' recognition and loyalty.

Here are the brand names and generic names for two of the psychiatric medications discussed in this book:

Depakote®	valproate
Prozac®	fluoxetine

limited to the realm of substance abuse, but influence how people perceive and treat impulse control disorders. Some people believe that just as a smoker should quit cold turkey, a person with an impulse control disorder should also be able to quit her behavior cold turkey.

metabolism: The chemical changes in the body that provide energy to the cells.

Luckily, the more modern medicine learns about the human brain and body, the more we realize that nothing humans do is as simple as pure, conscious decision making. Every action you take is influenced by millions of internal and external factors. Even a seemingly mundane action like getting out of bed in the morning is the result of numerous social, environmental, physical, and psychological factors. Your schedule for the day influences what time you decide to get up. The temperature, amount of sunlight, and weather conditions impact your body. The nutrients and substances from the things you eat and drink affect your metabolism.

Your daily schedule and your emotions and physical responses are linked.

Things like stress and emotions affect hormone balances. Your body is absorbing and reacting to all these conditions and more, creating an infinitely complex mix of physical and mental factors that will ultimately determine when you will wake and how you will feel when you get out of bed. Understanding that even simple daily decisions are part of a complicated web of physical and mental functions allows medical professionals to consider new perspectives and approaches when trying to understand more unusual behaviors like impulse control disorders.

The main treatment method for impulse control disorders has been psychiatric, or talk, therapy. In individual therapy sessions, patients attempt to identify the emotional sources of their behaviors. The hope is that once the patient knows why he is behaving in a certain way, he will be able to change that behavior. For example, let's consider Jerry's situation again. Perhaps in therapy Jerry would discuss how his parents were never around when Jerry was a child. Perhaps Jerry's parents never listened when he tried to talk to them, and his frustration with them would build up until he had an emotional explosion. Over time, Jerry may have learned that the only way to get their attention was to act out violently. He may then have become **acclimated** to this sort of behavior, beginning to strike out at smaller and smaller events. This behavior could become not only

acclimated: Became accustomed or used to something.

A child who feels ignored may learn inappropriate ways of coping with his emotions.

All of us have times when we cannot control our emotions; a person with an impulse control disorder experiences repeated bursts of uncontrollable emotion.

Drug Approval

Before a drug can be marketed in the United States, it must be officially approved by the Food and Drug Administration (FDA). Today's FDA is the primary consumer protection agency in the United States. Operating under the authority given it by the government, and guided by laws established throughout the twentieth century, the FDA has established a rigorous drug approval process that verifies the safety, effectiveness, and accuracy of labeling for any drug marketed in the United States.

While the United States has the FDA for the approval and regulation of drugs and medical devices, Canada has a similar organization called the Therapeutic Product Directorate (TPD). The TPD is a division of Health Canada, the Canadian government department of health. The TPD regulates drugs, medical devices, disinfectants, and sanitizers with disinfectant claims. Some of the things that the TPD monitors are quality, effectiveness, and safety. Just as the FDA must approve new drugs in the United States, the TPD must approve new drugs in Canada before those drugs can enter the market.

the way Jerry behaves when in an extremely stressful confrontation with his parents but also the way he responds to any unpleasant situation, no matter how insignificant. In therapy, Jerry could examine his past actions and begin to understand the different influences that caused his personality to develop in this way. Once Jerry knows the reasons for his behavior, he can work on taking control of that behavior.

The above scenario sounds simple, but the causes of most psychiatric disorders are much more complicated than this. As we discussed before, the mind and body are connected in very intricate ways, and most peoples' actions cannot be traced back to one factor.

There are numerous mental and physical factors affecting everything we do, and the best treatments are those that can address all of the factors influencing a person's behavior. Although some impulse control disorders might be treated most successfully through psychiatric therapy alone, there is growing evidence that there may also be chemical causes to these disorders. In such cases, medicines could be an important part of treatment.

One of the signs that impulse control disorders may have significant chemical influences is that many people with impulse control disorders suffer from coexisting disorders as well. For example, people with intermittent explosive disorder

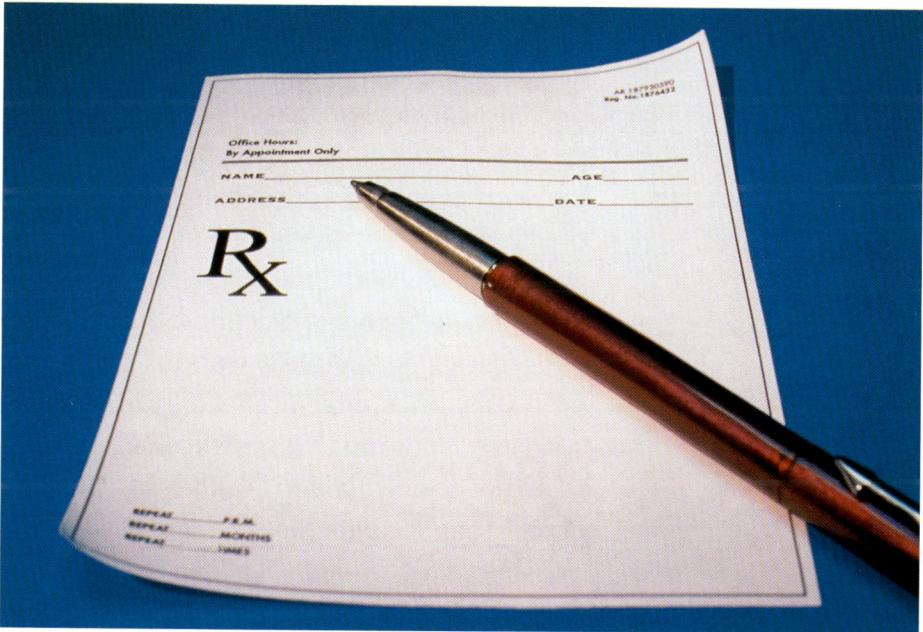

Prescription drugs may play a role in the treatment of individuals with impulse control disorders.

The FDA bases its approval on specific research results. Sometimes, a particular use for a drug may have been thoroughly researched by many studies, while other uses lack the same amount of research. In that case, the drug label will only include the uses that have met the FDA's stringent research requirements. Physicians, however, may continue to prescribe that drug for other "off-label" uses.

sometimes describe physical sensations like tremors and head pressure before an explosive episode. They may have a history of migraine headaches, poor coordination, altered serotonin metabolism, and other disorders like mood disorders, eating disorders, and substance abuse. People with kleptomania and trichotillomania also have a high incidence of coexisting disorders, especially eating disorders (like bulimia) and obsessive-compulsive disorder. Many people with pyromania are addicted to alcohol or have family histories of alcohol abuse, and people with pathological gambling often have histories of conditions such as hyperactive symptoms, mood disorders, and substance abuse. Recognizing these types of additional symptoms and conditions in people with impulse control disorders has helped researchers to identify possible drug treatments for these disorders. For example, some mood-stabilizing drugs, such as Depakote, have been shown to help people with migraine headaches. In such a case, a medical researcher may see that some people with intermittent explosive

bulimia: An eating disorder characterized by periods of binge eating followed by periods of purging, such as self-induced vomiting and the use of laxatives.

serotonin: A powerful neurotransmitter found especially in the brain.

disorder have a history of migraine headaches and mood disorders. The researcher may then think that, if this medication provides relief for mood disorders and migraine headaches, perhaps it will be helpful in treating intermittent explosive disorder as well. Depakote and other mood-stabilizing drugs have, in fact, helped some people with impulse control disorders like intermittent explosive disorder and pathological gambling.

At this time, there are no drugs that are approved by the United States Food and Drug Administration for the specific treatment of impulse control disorders. However, many international studies and anecdotal evidence suggest that certain psychiatric medications help patients with impulse control disorders, and research in this field is growing.

Most children are fascinated with firefighters, but a pyromaniac's preoccupation with fire may consume his entire life.

Chapter Three

How Some Psychiatric Drugs Work

Jeremiah's father was a fire fighter, and Jeremiah always wanted to be a fire fighter, too. But somehow, he knew he wasn't like his dad. His dad was a fire fighter because he wanted to protect people from fires. He went around to schools teaching kids about fire's destructive potential and how to protect themselves against fires. His father installed smoke detectors in every room of the house and checked the detectors once a month. Jeremiah's father hated fire and would do anything to prevent or stop it.

Jeremiah was very different from his dad. He wanted to be a fire fighter because he loved fire. He loved the way it looked, the way it smelled, how its heat enveloped everything, incinerating, eating, and destroying everything in its path. Jeremiah liked the smoke detectors in their house but not because they protected him from fires. He liked them because he loved taking them apart. Sometimes, after school, Jeremiah would sit in his room, dismantle the smoke detector piece by piece, and then put it back together. Once the smoke detector was reassembled, Jeremiah would light a match beneath it and time how many seconds it took before the detector let out its squeal.

For a long time, Jeremiah's parents laughed at his behavior. When he was small, they thought he was just trying to be like his dad. He loved the fire station, and when his father was off duty he would bring Jeremiah in to learn about the trucks, ladders, and fire equipment. His dad felt proud that Jeremiah had so much interest in

Many children will imitate their parents; Jeremiah's preoccupation with his father's job, however, went beyond what was normal or healthy.

A person with pyromania finds fire mesmerizing and may become lost in his obsession.

his job. After his father fought a fire, Jeremiah would beg to go to where the fire had been. Sometimes, if the fire had not been too severe, Jeremiah's dad would drive him to see the blackened building and tell Jeremiah what it had been like to fight the fire. Jeremiah sat paralyzed with awe while he listened to these stories. As his father spoke, Jeremiah saw the whole scene spread out before him almost as if he were there. Sometimes he would sneak back to the burned buildings alone to relive the story his dad had told. He loved the harsh scent of smoldering ash and burned paint.

As Jeremiah got older, his parents began to realize that his **preoccupation** with fire was much more than a healthy interest in his

> **preoccupation:** A state in which one's mind is absorbed in certain thoughts.

It is not always easy to understand why we behave the way we do. For example, has something good ever happened to one of your friends, like getting the lead in the school play or winning a large sum of money, and instead of feeling happy for her you were angry at her? This can be a very confusing situation for a person. Logically, you know that you should be happy for your friend and that your friend hasn't done anything wrong, but emotionally you just can't be happy. If you were to examine this emotional problem using psychotherapy, you might find that you are not really mad at your friend. The true reason you are angry is because you wish these good things would happen to you too. When you did not understand the reason you were upset, however, you turned your feelings of anger toward your friend. Now that you understand the real reason you are angry, you can try to be happy for your friend while still respecting your other emotions.

father's career. In fact, they began to realize that there was nothing healthy about Jeremiah's interest at all; it was an obsession. One day, Jeremiah's mother walked into his bedroom to find him seated on the floor staring intently at an old coffee can. Orange flames flickered out of the can, licking the wavy hot air above. Jeremiah stared, mesmerized. He had no idea that she was even in the room. Above Jeremiah's head, the smoke detector hung limply from loose red and blue wires.

Jeremiah's parents punished him for lighting the fire in the coffee can, but his strange behavior didn't stop. Two weeks later, the brush pile behind their house "mysteriously" caught fire. Not long after that, Jeremiah was caught pulling the fire alarm at school. After this incident, Jeremiah was forced to see a counselor. In his first session, Jeremiah tried to explain why he liked fire so much.

"I don't know why I do the things I do," he told his counselor. "I feel bad that my parents are so mad at me, but I don't feel bad about lighting the fire or pulling the fire alarm. Sometimes, it's hard for me to think— like my head is really full or something. But then I see some matches or a lighter. If I light a fire, it's like I can just stare into it, and I don't feel all confused and mixed up anymore. It's like all my bad thoughts go away. I can just look into the flame, and it eats up all my bad thoughts. Then I feel better again."

psychotherapy: An approach to treating mental disorders and emotional problems that focuses on teaching a person to discover, understand, and communicate their internal drives, motivations, and desires.

Jeremiah's counselor tried to explain all the reasons why Jeremiah shouldn't light fires. He explained that Jeremiah could hurt himself or other people. He said Jeremiah could get in big trouble with the law. He asked Jeremiah if he felt angry for some reason and if he was lighting fires to try to tell his parents that he was angry. Jeremiah thought the counselor's questions were stupid.

"My dad's a firefighter. I know all about fires. I already told you. I light fires because it makes me feel good."

Discussion

Traditional **psychotherapy** focuses on increasing a patient's awareness of her actions and understanding why she behaves this way. Psychotherapists believed that once the patient consciously understood her actions, she would be able to change these actions. In many types of psychiatric conditions, this approach is very successful. For example, a person may have severe anxiety that causes her to isolate herself from other people. Through therapy, she may tell her therapist about how she was abused as a child and how she used to hide in her room when her parents came home from work.

In some behavior modification therapy, the patient is taught to consider the consequences of his actions for himself and others. The patient may perform exercises designed to increase his sense of empathy. The hope is that if the patient understands the consequences of his actions, he will stop and think before performing those actions. In the case of impulse control disorders, however, if the person could simply stop performing the impulsive acts there would be no need to go to therapy. Although this method of increasing consideration and empathy is helpful for some people, it has little effect for others. When away from an impulsive situation, the patient knows that the action he is performing is negative and does not want to commit it. In Mary's story in chapter two, Mary knows that stealing is wrong and desperately wants to stop. But in the impulsive moment, she does not stop to think. It is as if her body and unconscious mind are working ahead of the conscious, decision-making mind. By the time she thinks about the consequences of the action, the action has already been performed.

She may then realize that the reason she has such high anxiety and remains isolated from people is because she is afraid of being hurt by the people around her. Once she realizes that her actions are motivated by fear, she can begin working on overcoming her fear and learning to live differently.

motivation: The cause or reason for performing an action.

For a long time, this type of psychotherapy and behavior modification remained the major approach to treating impulse control disorders. In the above story, Jeremiah's counselor is looking for the motivation behind Jeremiah's fire-starting. The counselor

Who can diagnose a psychiatric disorder?

- psychiatrists
- psychiatric advanced practice nurses
- medical doctors
- clinical nurse specialists
- nurse psychiatrists
- social workers
- psychologists

However, in most of the United States only medical doctors, psychiatrists, clinical nurse specialists, nurse psychiatrists, and advanced practice nurses can prescribe psychotropic medication.

believes that once Jeremiah understands why he is obsessed with fire and what the consequences of his obsession are, he will be able to stop himself from giving in to the impulse to light fires. However, traditional psychotherapy and behavior modification techniques often fail when used to treat pyromania and other impulse control disorders. The reason that this approach to therapy is often unsuccessful in treating these disorders is that these patients already have a conscious awareness of their actions but are still unable to change them. Many people in the medical field now believe that the reason patients cannot cease their impulsive acts is because these acts are not motivated by emotional and psychological causes; instead, their actions are caused by the way the patient's brain processes and responds to information.

In *Handbook of Childhood Impulse Disorders and ADHD*, Dr. Koziol explains that different areas of the brain are responsible for processing different types of information. For example, one part of the brain

A Neuron

Dendrites

Cell Body

Dendrites

Axon's Terminal Button

Axon

Synapse

Neurotransmitters

Receptors

Terminal Button

Cell Body

Dendrite of another Cell

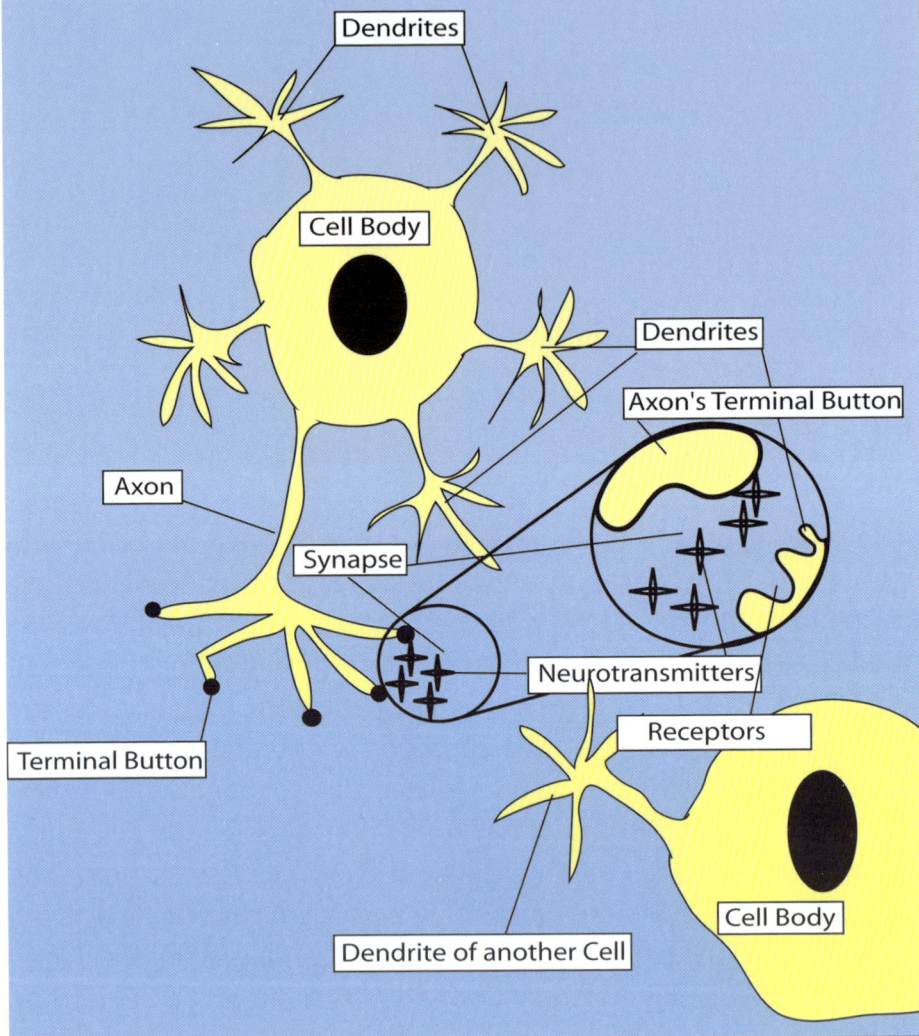

Neurotransmitters deliver messages from one nerve cell to the next.

is responsible for long-term memory. Another part of the brain is responsible for short-term memory. When you are learning a new lesson, a certain area of your brain becomes active. When you are engaged in physical activity, a different part of your brain is working. In order for you to function properly, all these different parts of your brain must communicate and share information with each other.

If you learned a new lesson today about the proper way to behave on a date and wanted to use that information to figure out what went wrong on your failed date last week, you would need the learning part of your brain to communicate with the memory part of your brain. Or imagine that your younger sibling does something to make you really angry, like ruins your favorite piece of clothing or rips every page out of your favorite book. The parts of your brain responsible for reactions and reflexes may surge to strike out at your sibling. The parts of your brain, however, that are responsible for learning lessons and maintaining beliefs and values access your belief that hurting others is wrong. The different parts of your brain then communicate all these messages to each other, and you decide to take a deep breath and control your urge to hurt your sibling.

neurotransmitters: Chemicals that carry messages from one nerve cell to another.

Dr. Koziol suggests that people with disorders like obsessive-compulsive disorder, attention-deficit disorder, and impulse control disorders have a lack of communication between these different areas of the brain. For example, the learning part of Jeremiah's brain knows that setting fires is wrong, but this part of his brain might not be able to communicate this belief to other parts of his brain. When the part of his brain that controls actions sends a message to light a fire, the thinking part of his brain cannot intervene to stop the message.

Messages sent between different parts of the brain are sent using neurotransmitters. If the brain is not communicating properly,

One of the hormones that floods your body during a sympathetic nervous response is adrenaline. Adrenaline is the same hormone that rushes through wild animals' bodies when they are under attack. This hormone gives them a sudden burst of strength that can mean the difference between life and death. If adrenaline levels in a person, however, stay high, the person will have difficulty functioning in normal situations, because the brain has turned off thinking and the body has turned on to either fight or run.

it could be the result of an imbalance of neurotransmitters or a malfunction in the parts of the nerve cells that pick up neurotransmitters. In such a case, medications might be helpful in reestablishing the balance of neurotransmitters within the brain or affecting the receptor sites so that they can receive the neurotransmitters. Using medications in this way has been extremely useful in treating some psychiatric illnesses like depression, anxiety, and bipolar disorder, and doctors hope that it will be helpful in treating impulse control disorders as well.

To date, the type of psychiatric medication that seems most promising for the treatment of impulse control disorders is selective serotonin reuptake inhibitors (SSRIs). SSRIs are the most commonly prescribed antidepressants. The neurotransmitter serotonin plays an important part in the communication between different regions of the brain. How well different regions of the brain are able to communicate with each other seems to influence the way we behave.

In their book, *Anger Kills: Seventeen Strategies for Controlling the Hostility That Can Harm Your Health*, Redford Williams and Virginia Williams discuss the effects of low serotonin levels on how people express anger. Their book describes a condition that they call the Hostility Syndrome, a condition similar to intermittent explosive disorder. Much of what they discuss could also be applied to impulse

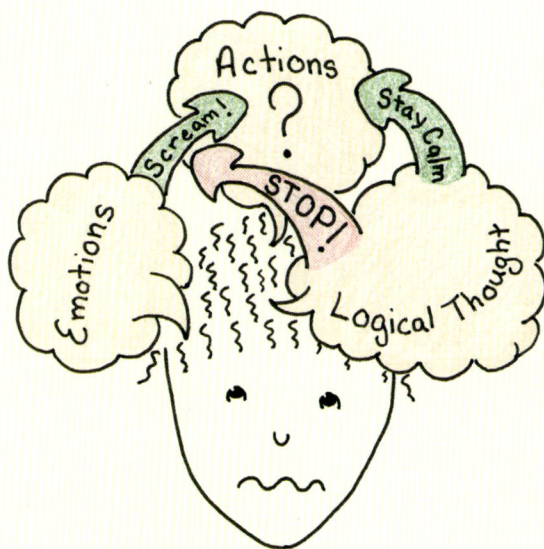

The mental processes that lead to emotions, actions, and logical thought are all interconnected.

control disorders. They explain that people with a high tendency toward aggressive and hostile behavior appear to have highly active sympathetic nervous systems and underactive parasympathetic nervous systems. Serotonin seems to play a large role in how these different parts of the nervous system function and communicate.

The sympathetic nervous system is responsible for the "flight or fight" response within the body—the immediate impulses you feel when faced with a stressful or dangerous situation. The parasympathetic nervous system balances, slows, and blocks the effects of the sympathetic nervous system in the body. For example, if you felt threatened by a person at school, your sympathetic nervous system would flood your body with hormones in preparation for a fight or a quick retreat. However, you know that it is better to solve problems calmly and rationally, so your parasympathetic nervous system would begin sending other messages to block the fight or flight response and calm your system. One theory about the role of these

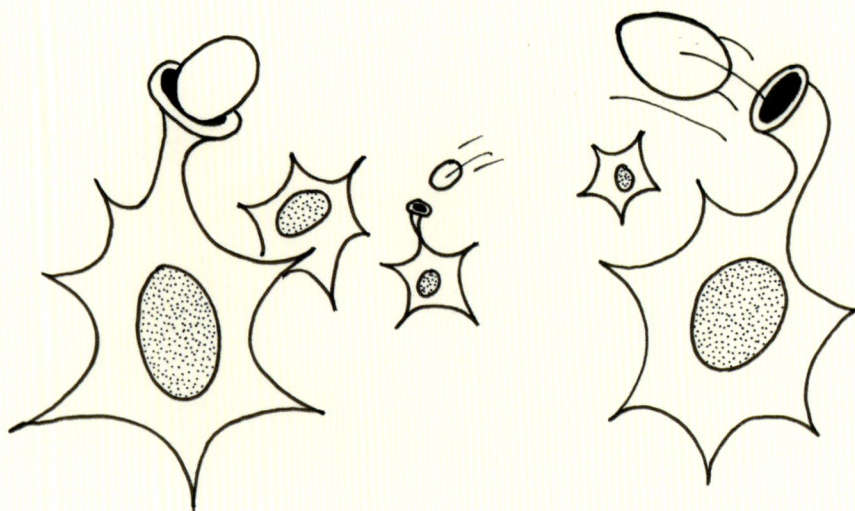

Serotonin helps neurons deliver their messages from one to another.

systems in impulse control disorders is that the sense of tension that patients describe feeling prior to committing an impulsive act could be the result of an overactive sympathetic nervous system. The sense of relief they feel after committing the impulsive act may be caused by the impulsive action "kick starting" the parasympathetic nervous response.

Serotonin plays an important part in relaying the messages of the parasympathetic nervous system to the sympathetic nervous system. A person with too little serotonin tends to have an overactive sympathetic nervous system and underactive parasympathetic system, leading to a greater tendency toward impulsive behavior. Too little serotonin can also affect our moods, sleep, eating habits, learning, and many other important functions.

Some people have low serotonin levels because the cells that produce serotonin begin to reabsorb the serotonin before it can go out and perform its job in the body. Though it is not clear exactly how SSRIs work, SSRIs like Prozac, Paxil, Zoloft, Celexa, and Luvox appear to keep these cells from reabsorbing the serotonin. Preventing reabsorption allows the serotonin to stay in the body longer, hopefully leading to an increase in serotonin levels and an improvement in the patient's quality of life. SSRIs are prescribed to people with clinical depression because balancing serotonin levels helps to regulate a person's mood, but SSRIs have also helped people control eating disorders, alcoholism, smoking, aggressive behaviors, and obsessive-compulsive disorder (a disorder that shares many similarities with impulse control disorders).

People with impulse control disorders commonly develop clinical depression in addition to their other disorder; therefore, a doctor may wish to prescribe an antidepressant for this coexisting condition. Some antidepressants, however, can cause increased anxiety in the patient. Patients with impulse control disorders mention tension and anxiety as one of the factors that trigger their impulses, so doctors must be careful to determine that a medication meant to be helpful will not end up making the patient's condition even worse. SSRIs tend to be a good choice should medication be needed because they have a low incidence of anxiety-producing side effects.

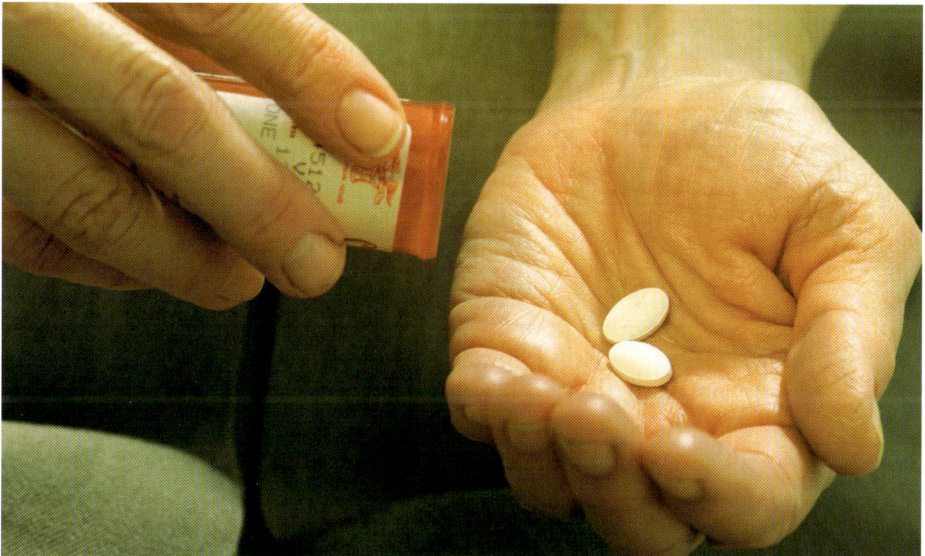

SSRIs are the most promising drugs for the treatment of impulse control disorders.

Researchers are looking for new and better ways to treat psychiatric disorders pharmaceutically.

Although SSRIs seem to be the most promising drug treatment for impulse control disorders, the class of psychiatric medications known as mood stabilizers has also helped some people with impulse control disorders. Mood stabilizers are a group of drugs used to treat conditions such as mania and bipolar disorder. These drugs are also helpful in treating people with intermittent explosive disorder and pathological gambling disorder. Some of these drugs are also effective in the treatment of additional disorders like epilepsy and migraine headaches. It is not clear how most mood stabilizers, like lithium and risperidone, produce their therapeutic effects. These drugs influence the chemical balance in the brain, but researchers do not yet know exactly how the drugs change chemical balances and why these changes affect behavior.

mania: This is a bipolar disorder in which a person feels an exaggerated feeling of elation, inflated self-esteem, and hyperactivity.

epilepsy: A neurologic disorder characterized with periodic physical or sensory seizures.

A person with an impulse control disorder may suffer from a
number of destructive impulses.

Chapter Four

Treatment Description

Pilar had been pulling her hair, biting her nails, and picking at her skin since she was a little girl. At first her parents thought it was just a habit she would outgrow, but she never did. Pilar tried everything to stop these habits. She painted her nails so that they would taste bad if she bit them; she bit them anyway. She wore gloves, but then she chewed on those. She wrapped her head in tight scarves so that all her hair was covered and tied away, but then she pulled at her eyebrows and eyelashes instead. She planned a system of rewards and punishments for herself: if she went all day without biting, picking, or pulling, she could eat, but if she gave in to her impulses, she wouldn't allow herself to touch food. This "reward system" grew into a serious eating disorder that made all of Pilar's problems worse.

Pilar hated the way she looked. She was so thin it seemed like she would collapse, but she still felt fat. She felt depressed all the time and didn't want to get out of bed. When she looked in the mirror, she was repulsed by the shiny, red patches where hair should have been. She refused to go to school because of the way she looked. Pilar's parents didn't know what to do, but when she stopped going to school, they made her see a psychiatrist.

Pilar's psychiatrist said he thought her depression and eating disorder where based on her inability to control her hair pulling and nail-biting impulses. He said what had started as a small problem had gone out of control. He thought that if they could control her trichotillomania, it would be easier to treat her depression and eating disorder.

Pilar and her psychiatrist began behavior modification therapy. Pilar worked on learning the warning signs that preceded pulling hair or biting nails. For example, she often felt short of breath and nervous before pulling her hair. Pilar's psychiatrist helped her develop ways to stay calm and try to separate herself from these impulse-triggering feelings. Pilar concentrated on creating a "safe room" in her mind. Sometimes she would imagine herself in this room, protected from her negative feelings. On some occasions, Pilar found that if she began meditating as soon as she felt the slightest nervousness, she could stop the impulse to pull her hair before it started. At other times, however, trying to resist the urge to pull her hair made her feel even more tense and desperate. Her psychiatrist suggested that at times like these, instead of trying to resist the impulse, Pilar should concentrate on doing something else to keep her hands busy. This way, she could modify her impulses from hair pulling into less damaging activities.

One of the things Pilar did was buy a book on origami. When she began feeling nervous or short of breath, Pilar would reach for a piece of paper and fold it instead of pulling her hair. This way, she found she could keep her hands busy until the impulse passed. After a while, Pilar could fold a paper crane in seconds. She also did other things to keep her hands busy, like tearing paper, twisting yarn, and

Pilar had to learn new ways to handle her impulses. Her psychiatrist helped her develop new strategies that were constructive rather than destructive.

Origami is the Japanese art of folding paper into animals, flowers, and other decorative shapes. Human beings have always used art as a way to express their feelings. More and more therapists are finding that art can be an important part of therapy. Patients can often draw, paint, or use other artwork to express the feelings for which they don't have words. Many people also find the process of creating art to be calming, meditative, and therapeutic. For some patients, creating artwork helps them not only to express their feelings about a certain situation but also to soothe their emotions and calm their minds.

knitting; these strategies seemed to be working. Her psychiatrist explained to her, however, that what they were practicing was not a cure. He said she was learning to simply replace one impulsive action with another, and although this might help her resist pulling her hair, in the long run she might not gain the relief she needed from this sort of substitution.

For a long time, however, Pilar was happy with her treatment. She felt so relieved to see hair growing back on the crown of her head and the nape of her neck that she didn't mind the constant paper folding, tearing, and knitting. After a few months, however, she began to realize what her psychiatrist had been trying to explain. Even though she was no longer pulling out her hair, the uncomfortable feelings of tension and anxiety that caused her impulses still plagued her. Furthermore, her feelings of depression had returned and were now as strong as they had been when she first began therapy. She was still battling her eating disorder as well. Breathing deeply, meditating, and doing things with her hands definitely helped her resist pulling her hair, but she wished she could stop feeling this internal panic and turmoil completely. She asked her doctor what else he could suggest, and he explained that maybe it was time to consider trying a medication. He explained to Pilar that treatment would be a long and difficult road with ups and downs. She might never find a total cure for her condition, but by finding the right balance of therapy, behavior modification, and medication she could live a normal and happy life.

Discussion

The major treatment for impulse control disorders is psychotherapy focused on behavior modification. Psychotherapy is a very individual treatment, and each person's treatment plan will be different. Nevertheless, there are some helpful basic guidelines that many therapists follow when creating a treatment program, regardless of the disorder for which the patient is being treated.

The first and most important step in therapy is to establish a secure environment for the patient. The therapist's office should be a place of trust where the patient feels encouraged to freely discuss physical and emotional matters that may be confusing, embarrass-

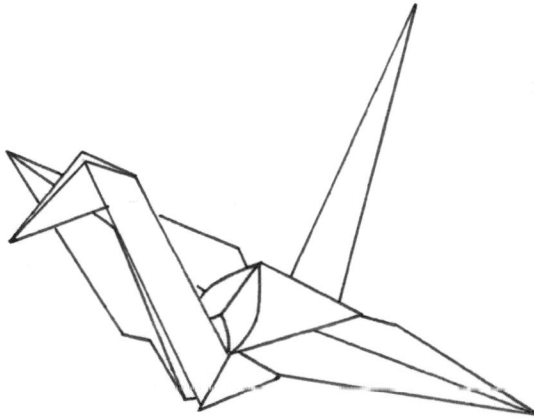

Origami provides a constructive way to occupy hands when a person with trichotillomania feels the urge to pull her hair.

A therapist should provide a secure environment.

ing, guilt inducing, frightening, or otherwise uncomfortable. The patient should feel both physically and emotionally safe. In the above story, Pilar also creates a safe place in her mind. Many therapists use this technique to help their patients create a sanctuary where they can go when they are away from the therapist's office. As in Pilar's experience, this safe place is usually a room that the patient can imagine going to when she feels threatened. The patient fills this "inner" or "mental" room with comforting objects and soothing imagery. Therapists might instruct the patient to imagine a strong lock on the door of the room so that she can keep bad thoughts or painful emotions from entering.

Defining and developing boundaries is another important step in beginning the treatment process. Many therapists believe there should be no physical contact between the doctor and the patient. Setting clear guidelines at the beginning of therapy regarding physical contact can help make the therapist's office a safe space. Therapists should also establish guidelines for telephone availability. Most therapists make themselves available by telephone for emergency

A person can create an imaginary "safe place," somewhere she can retreat mentally when she feels anxious or tense.

A psychiatrist can provide pharmaceutical treatment combined with other forms of therapy.

situations only. Too much reliance on telephone conversation can have an adverse affect on the therapeutic doctor–patient relationship. If a patient calls her therapist every time she feels uncomfortable or confused, she will not learn how to overcome difficulties on her own.

Treatment scheduling is also an important part of defining the boundaries of therapy. Most therapists see patients for fifty minutes each week. When a person begins to see improvements from therapy, she may want to spend more time with her therapist and have more frequent sessions. This can be damaging in the long run. If a patient is unstable or in danger of harming herself or others, a short period of time in which therapy sessions are held more frequently may be helpful. Once a patient is stabilized, however, it is important to maintain a regular treatment schedule so that the patient does not become overly dependent on her therapist. Although psychiatric therapy can last a long time—even years—in most cases it is not meant to be a lifelong activity. Eventually, the patient will move beyond therapy, and when this happens, the patient must know that she can maintain good mental health on her own without her therapist's help.

Once a safe place and boundaries for therapy have been established, the doctor and patient should discuss the goals of therapy. Over the course of treatment, patients and therapists should periodically review the goals of the treatment program. Checking in on goals can help patients determine if they are making progress. Additionally, the goals one begins with when starting therapy may change over time. One might realize that a specific goal is unreasonable for her time frame. One might also find that she surpassed a goal long ago and that it is time to set new goals. In Pilar's story, we see that her original goal was simply to stop pulling her hair. She was quite pleased with the progress she made in achieving this goal. However, over time Pilar found that she wanted more changes in her life, so she and her doctor revisited the goals of her therapy program and discussed options for Pilar's next step.

For most people with psychiatric disorders, therapy is a process that has both ups and downs. Sometimes a patient will make exciting progress, but there will probably also be frustrating relapses or backward steps. Expectations for therapy should be reasonable and flexible. Patients should understand that needing to alter goals or slow the pace of therapy is in no way a failure; it is simply an adjustment for their current needs.

The major goal of a patient seeking treatment for an impulse control disorder would be to cease their impulsive actions. This, however, is not as easy to do as it may sound. Pilar has tried many times to cease pulling her hair, but her attempts to stop pulling led to even bigger problems like an eating disorder. A much more helpful goal for patients with impulse control disorders is to stop the impulse

A person with a psychiatric disorder cannot continuously sweep his difficulties under the carpet; they need to be confronted before they can get better.

An individual's interior mental processes are often mysterious and confusing. Neither therapy nor medication can provide all the answers—but they can work together to make things more clear.

Therapy has ups and downs.

before it starts. The patient might work on discovering what types of things trigger the impulse and then find ways to avoid those things or react to them in a different way. If Pilar meditates as soon as she feels nervous, she can often avoid feeling the impulse to pull her hair. If a patient with intermittent explosive disorder realizes he always feels tightness in his throat and buzzing in his head before an explosive episode, then he might work on becoming more sensitive to and aware of those bodily sensations. Then, when he feels these sensations starting, he can leave the room, meditate, or otherwise separate himself from the situation before he gets any closer to exploding.

precursors: Things that come before and indicate the approach of something else.

As we see in Pilar's story, behavior modification therapy does not just concentrate on identifying the precursors to impulsive actions, but also on how to deal with the impulsive feelings once they start. Pilar still feels driven to impulsive behaviors, but part of her treatment is learning to perform a different, less damaging action. Instead of pulling her hair, she habitually folds paper. This method of behavior modification can be extremely beneficial for some people, allowing them to channel their impulsive energy from negative actions into positive actions. This method of behavior modification also has its drawbacks, however, in that the patient is not necessarily becoming less impulsive; she is just substituting one impulsive behavior for another.

If a patient, in consultation with his doctor, decides that medication might be a helpful addition to his psychiatric therapy, he will have to follow the treatment program carefully. In the case of impulse control disorders, the doctor would probably begin by prescribing

A person with an impulse control disorder needs to identify the triggers that "light her fuse."

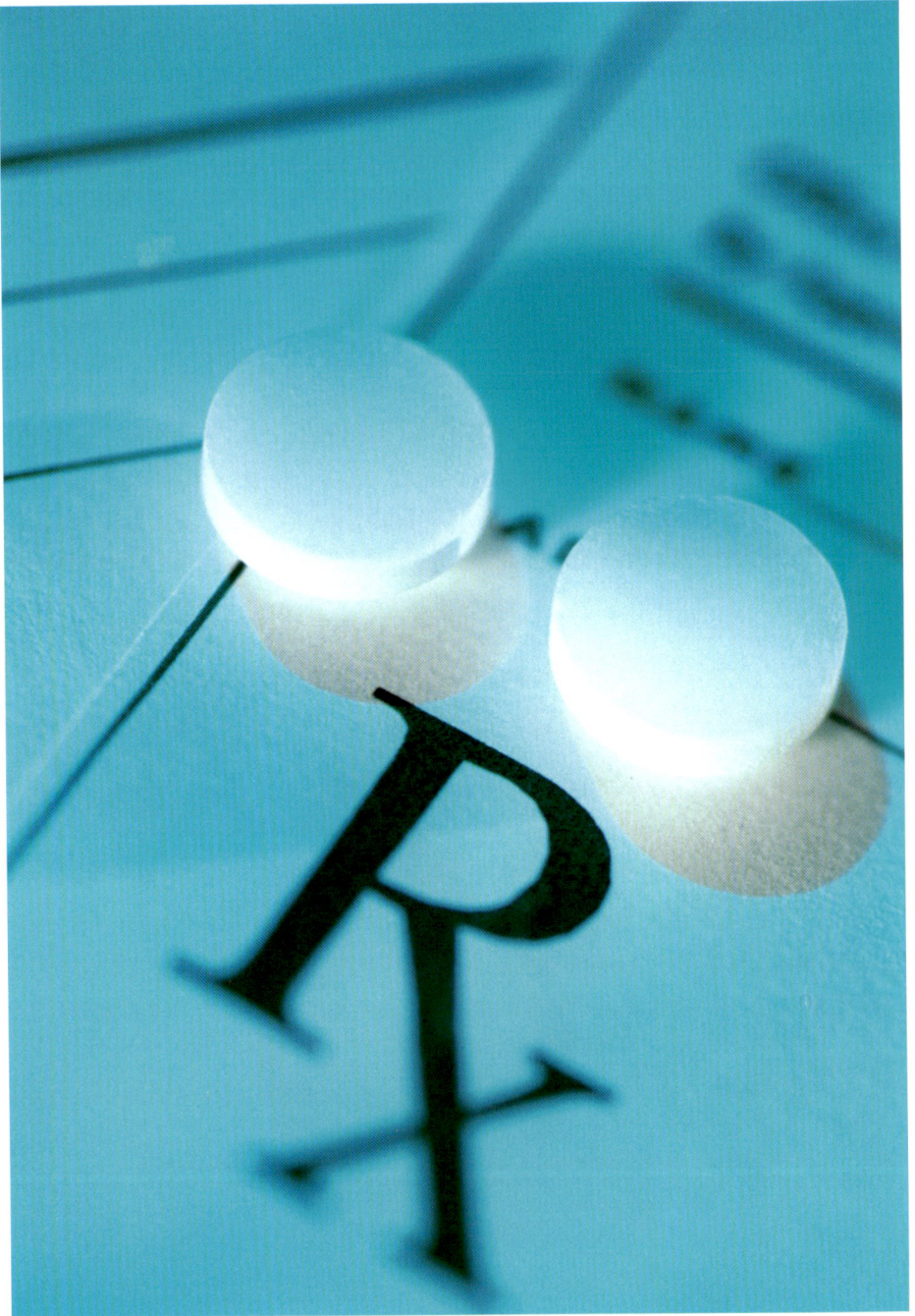

Medication may be a helpful supplement to therapy for a person with an impulse control disorder.

an SSRI. There are a number of different SSRIs, and it would be up to the doctor to decide which of these medications to prescribe. Doctors usually begin by prescribing the medication that has the lowest rate of side effects. However, not every drug works for every person, so a patient may need to try a number of different drugs before finding the one that is right for him. Although some people feel relief within three weeks after beginning drug treatment, it can take as long as eight to ten weeks for psychiatric medications to begin taking effect.

Many psychiatric drugs require a weaning-on period—a period of time when the patient takes a smaller than average dose so that her body can get used to the medication. This may affect the amount of time it takes for the patient to experience any benefit from the drug. For example, the typical therapeutic dose for the SSRI Zoloft is 50 milligrams once each day. However, a patient who is just beginning to take Zoloft would generally begin by taking a 25-milligram dose once each day so that her body can adjust to the medication. After one week, the dosage should be increased. For some people, 50 milligrams of Zoloft is still too little to produce a therapeutic effect. In this case, the doctor would slowly increase the dosage up to a maximum of 200 milligrams per day. The amount of time it takes for a patient's body to adjust to a therapeutic dose will affect how long it is before the patient notices any benefits from taking the medication.

Some psychiatric medications, like Depakote for example, are metabolized by the liver and need to be monitored to protect against

therapeutic dose: The amount of medication that provides a positive effect for the patient. For example, a child would only need a small amount of Tylenol to treat her symptoms, but an adult would require a much larger amount.

metabolized: To be changed within the body. When your body metabolizes food, it breaks the food down into nutrients for different parts of the body (calcium for your bones, sugars for energy) and waste products that exit the body.

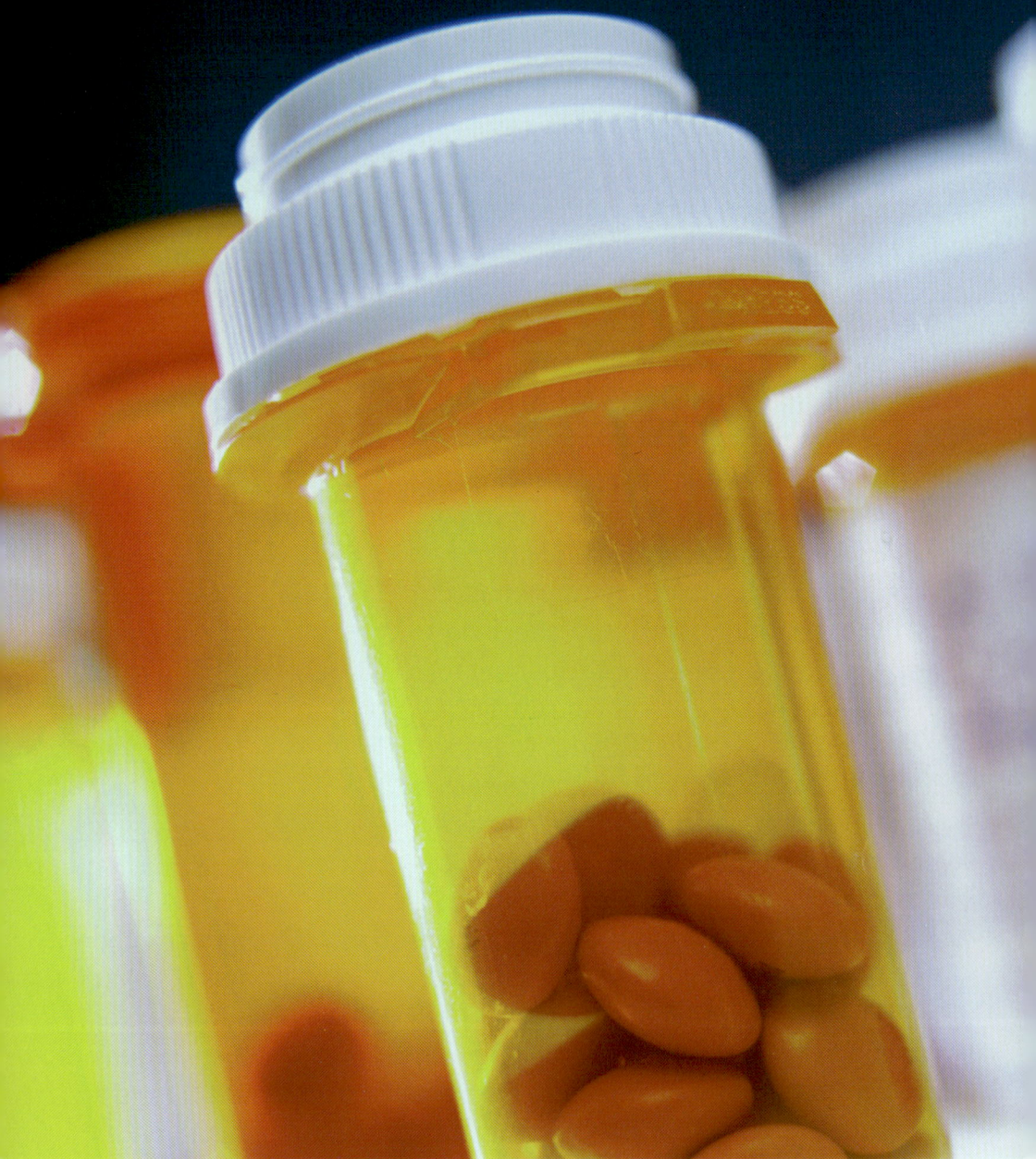

A person with an impulse control disorder may receive medication for a coexisting disorder.

liver damage. When beginning a medication like this, the doctor will require routine blood tests to measure how well the patient's body is metabolizing the drug. At first, the doctor may require blood tests as often as every two weeks; then she will gradually extend the testing period to once every one to three months. For some patients, the medication may help their psychiatric disorder but may begin to damage the liver or other parts of the body. In such a case, the doctor and patient must decide which presents a more immediate threat, the psychiatric disorder or the medication. In almost all cases in which a medication is threatening liver health or function, the patient must stop taking the medication and look for other medications to help her disorder. However, there can be great dangers in ceasing medications suddenly. Just as many psychiatric medications have a weaning-on period, many also have a weaning-off period in which the patient gradually reduces her daily dosage, allowing her body to adjust before ending the medication completely.

People with impulse control disorders often have coexisting disorders like obsessive-compulsive disorder, depression, or anxiety. In some cases, patients are prescribed medications for these coexisting disorders. It is important to remember that treating a coexisting disorder is not the same thing as treating the primary impulse control disorder. Pilar suffers from an eating disorder and depression in addition to her trichotillomania. If her psychiatrist, however, only treated her depression by giving her an antidepressant, he would not be treating the trichotillomania that led to her becoming depressed in the first place. Sometimes, though, treating coexisting disorders with medications can make it easier for a patient to undergo therapy. For example, if Pilar is so depressed that she cannot concentrate on anything else, then her therapy won't help her trichotillomania. If she can bring her depression under control with medication, she may be able to focus on her therapy and make greater strides in overcoming her other disorders.

Whereas some people find that once the source of their impulse control disorder is treated, they are able to proceed without

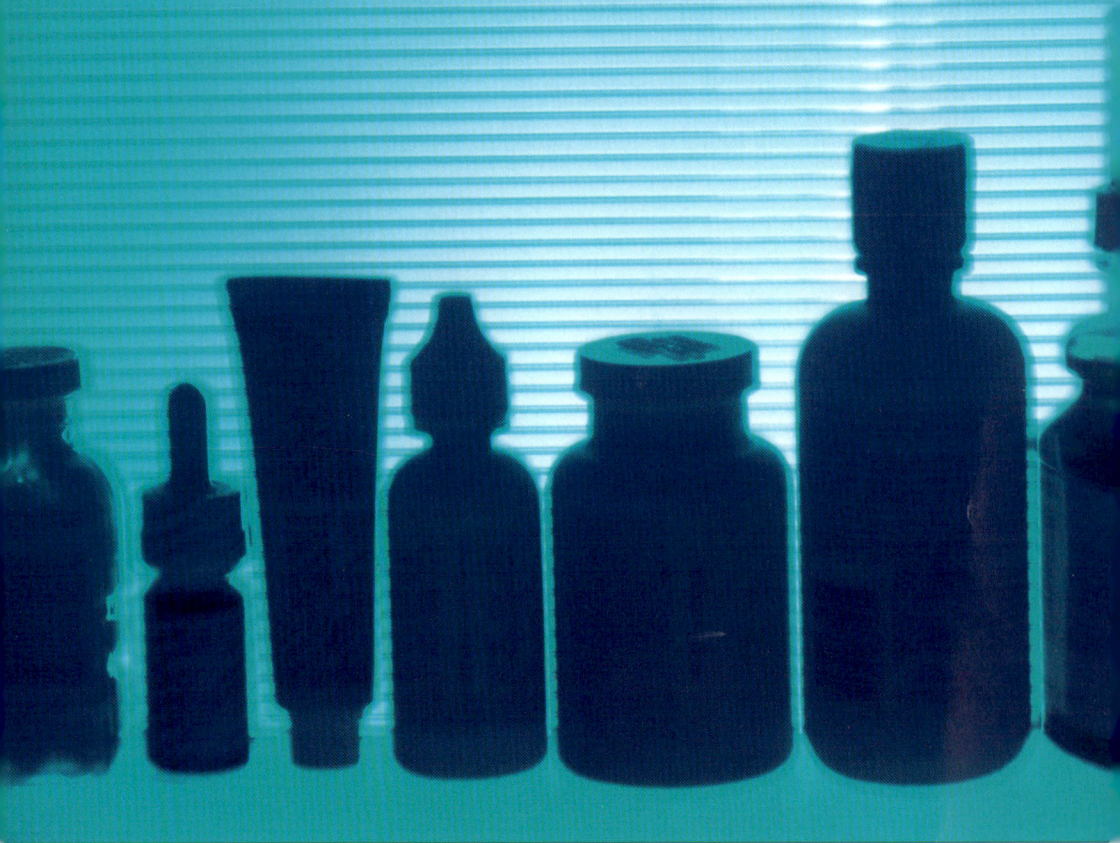

Medicine can provide long-term help for many medical conditions.

medications, others may find that medications are a necessity in the ongoing maintenance of good health. Perhaps a patient with trichotillomania is able to stop hair pulling through psychiatric therapy but nevertheless has a coexisting mood disorder like depression that makes medication a necessary part of the rest of her life.

Many people, not just those with psychiatric conditions, live and thrive because of the help of medication. People with conditions like severe asthma and diabetes must always take medication to maintain good health. Long-term medication for psychiatric conditions can be considered in the same way.

Pathological gambling is a form of impulse control disorder.

Case Studies

We can better understand impulse control disorders when we look at real-life people who experience these psychological conditions. These people are not "crazy" or "nuts"—nor are they "bad" or "immoral." Instead, they suffer from a physical and emotional condition that causes certain unacceptable and often destructive behaviors.

A Case Study in Pathological Gambling

Jose had been gambling for years, and his life was a mess. His wife had threatened to divorce him three years before when he gam-

A common misconception about psychiatric drugs, especially antidepressants like Prozac, is that they make you feel happy all the time. Unlike some illegal drugs like cocaine that give a person a false and temporary feeling of strength, elation, or invincibility, psychiatric drugs balance chemicals within the body so that a person's emotions exist within a more normal range. A person taking an antidepressant like Prozac will still feel normal emotions like sadness and disappointment, but it will not be the same type of immobilizing depression that a chemical imbalance can cause.

bled away all their savings at a casino in Niagara Falls. When he gave her the news, she cried and screamed and threatened to leave, but he stopped her. He promised that he would never do it again, that he would make it up to her and seek help. He looked for a support group and got a second job. But he still felt like the hurt and mistrust was always there. He knew, however, that they could make it through the hard times if he could keep his word. Eventually his wife would forgive him.

Four months later, Jose received an unexpected Christmas bonus at work. At first he was thrilled that he could bring this extra money home to his wife. But then he got an idea. He thought about taking the money to the casino. He felt sure he could make this money even bigger. Maybe he could win enough to make up for everything he'd lost. He thought about how great it would be to be able to replace the savings he'd gambled away. Then his marriage and his life could go back to being normal and healthy.

The scene in the casino was a living nightmare. First he lost the Christmas bonus, and then he lost all the money from his last two paychecks. Going home that night, Jose felt sick and anxious. He couldn't talk to anyone. He snapped at his son, slammed doors all around the house, brooded in the living room with all the lights off, and paced around the kitchen all night long. The next day he made a fateful decision. He was going to win that money back, but he needed money in order to do it. In desperation, he took all the money from his son's college fund. Then he went to the casino and lost all that money too.

That was when his wife left him. Since then, Jose has tried to stop gambling many times, but he never could. He gambled when he was happy, which was seldom, and he gambled when he was depressed, which was most of the time. He lost both of his jobs. After he repeatedly borrowed money and never paid it back, his friends abandoned him as well. Jose felt there was nothing left to live for; he even began contemplating suicide.

Poker is just one form of gambling.

Pathological gambling can lead to depression and other psychiatric conditions.

Finally, in financial ruin and emotional desperation, Jose decided to see a doctor. Jose felt like therapy was his last hope. When his doctor prescribed Prozac, Jose was very skeptical. He didn't see how a little pill could fix his depression or make him stop gambling, and he was right. The doctor explained to him that the pills couldn't do any of those things but that they could help regulate the chemicals within his brain. The doctor told Jose that this wouldn't make his problems go away, but that it might help him face his problems and control his impulses when they started.

For many weeks, Jose didn't notice anything at all. He was still depressed. He still gambled, and he still wondered what in life he had to look forward to. But after a while, things seemed to slowly improve. Jose had gotten a new job, and one day he noticed that he was able to concentrate for longer periods of time at work. He felt like he was opening up more and sharing more with his therapist. For the first time, he thought he was beginning to understand the impulses in his body; he realized these impulses would continue to come but they would also go. Now, when he felt the need to gamble, he did other things to distract himself. He'd call a member of his support group to talk until he calmed down. He would sit down with his journal and write all the reasons he shouldn't gamble; at the end of that long list, he wouldn't want to gamble anymore. After a while, he found he needed to do this less and less. He couldn't explain why exactly, but he felt like he was gaining control of his pathological gambling and his life.

A Case Study in
Intermittent Explosive Disorder

When Donna was a child, her parents described her as "a little terror." They always said this jokingly, but Donna definitely had her troubling side. She was hyperactive, easily distracted, and prone to temper tantrums. Now, as a teenager, she was still having troubles.

Until recently, Donna's parents had attributed her behavior to the general moodiness, hormone fluctuations, and rebelliousness of the teenage years. Now, with her behavior growing worse, it was becoming more and more apparent that Donna's actions weren't simply a phase. Her mother even began to notice a disturbing pattern to Donna's behavior. It seemed like every few weeks Donna would get a series of terrible headaches. Donna said these headaches made her feel nauseous, as if there were pressure building up, ready to explode. For the next few days after Donna got headaches like these, everyone walked on eggshells because anything could send Donna into a rage. She would scream, break things, and even strike out at other people. After these episodes, Donna would be depressed and exhausted. She would lock herself in her bedroom and hardly come out for two to three days. When Donna finally emerged from her room, she acted happy and normal as if nothing had ever happened.

Impulse control disorders are often confused with normal adolescent moodiness and rebellion.

A person with intermittent explosive disorder loses her temper easily. She may scream, break things, or become violent to others.

The family could relax and feel ordinary for a few weeks until the headaches surfaced again.

It was more a relief than a shock when a psychiatrist diagnosed Donna with intermittent explosive disorder. In a psychiatric evaluation, Donna told the doctor about the headaches that preceded her angry outbursts and about the fatigue and depression she felt afterward. Because she had these additional symptoms, the psychiatrist thought that it might be helpful to supplement Donna's therapy with medication.

The psychiatrist explained to Donna that Depakote, a medication usually used to treat mania and seizures, had been shown to also help people with migraine headaches and bipolar disorder. Bipolar disorder, she explained, was a psychiatric disorder in which a person experienced manic episodes followed by deeply depressed states. She told Donna that, although she was not suffering from bipolar disorder, some of her symptoms—her loss of control followed by fatigue and guilt—were similar and that Depakote might help her situation as well.

Donna has entered a period of intense treatment consisting of therapy, Depakote, and family counseling. In therapy, she works on developing ways to control her anger, like learning how to breathe deeply, imagining herself in a calm and pleasant place, and counting backward from one hundred when she feels annoyed. Donna is also finding that therapy, by just providing a person to talk to, has helped her to understand her emotions and explore other ways to deal with her frustration.

Family counseling is helping both Donna and her parents. In family counseling, Donna has begun to realize that she doesn't always consider how her actions affect those around her. Donna's parents are learning that they can do things to help Donna when she is feeling stressed or sick before the situation escalates into an explosion.

Although it is still too soon to tell, Donna thinks that the Depakote is helping her headaches. She still gets them, but they don't seem as severe and they don't happen as frequently; she is thankful for this change. Another pleasant change happened one day when Donna was feeling particularly depressed and tired after an explosive episode. Donna was sure that her parents were upset and deeply disappointed, but then they surprised her by going to the local animal shelter and bringing home a kitten! Even when Donna is frustrated and angry with everyone else, when the fuzzy little cat jumps on her lap, Donna feels soothed and calmed.

One of the most important strides Donna and her family have made in treatment is understanding that Donna is not acting out ag-

Physical well-being is important to psychiatric balance.

A pet may help an individual better handle destructive impulses.

Donna says that having a cat helps her to manage her impulse control disorder better. Do pets have healing powers? Some doctors say they do! Studies suggest that people who have pets may have fewer mental disorders, recover from illness and surgery faster, and stay healthier longer. Doctors believe that these health benefits result from the fact that pets are a source of love and comfort, and that people who have pets feel they have a reason to stay healthy. Pets can be especially important for elderly people and people who do not have family living close by. Some nursing homes have even begun bringing pets in to live among the residents. The vast majority of residents living in these homes report that having pets improves their quality of life.

gressively because she wants to or because she hates her parents, but because she has a medical condition that they are all learning to understand.

The cost of medication and other medical treatments may be high in terms of money—but there may be other physical and psychological costs that have to be weighed carefully as well.

Chapter Six

Risks and Side Effects

Marcus took lithium for two years. It helped him to control his obsessive thoughts and impulses to light fires, but it had other effects as well. A few months into his treatment, he developed a tremor in his hand. His doctor told him that this side effect wasn't dangerous and would probably go away on its own. The tremor never went away, and even though he knew it wasn't harmful, it still made Marcus uncomfortable and self-conscious. He felt like people looked at him strangely, like somehow they could tell what was going on in his mind when they saw this tremor in his hand.

Marcus had other physical symptoms as well. He often felt nauseous and tired. He spent a lot more time sleeping than he ever had before. Even when he was awake, he never felt fully aware. It was almost as if he was walking through a fog, like there was a wall of glass between him and the things going on around him. Colors seemed duller, sounds seemed muffled, and smells seemed blunted, as if he had a cold or stuffy head. He always felt a little further away than he should be.

The side effects that bothered Marcus weren't just physical. He felt like the medication affected his daily life as well. He had to check with his doctor often to monitor and adjust his lithium levels. This constant need for medical check-ups made him lose time from work and feel like his life was a series of doctor's visits. He found that re-membering to take the medication also posed difficulties. Already prone to obsessive thoughts, Marcus would sometimes take his medication but then be unable to remember if he had taken it or not. Sometimes he knew that he had taken the medication, but he still couldn't stop obsessing about the slight possibility that maybe he had made a mistake. Finally, Marcus decided that the side effects

Like dynamite, psychiatric medicines can be used for construc-tive purposes—but they can also be extremely dangerous.

Our minds can do powerful things. For example, in medical research doctors gave sick patients something ordinary, like sugar pills, but told the patients that they were receiving powerful medication. Some of the patients who were given the sugar pills got better. Scientists determined that the patients were cured simply because they believed that the medicine would cure them. What cured the patients was not the pill but the power of their own minds and bodies. This is called the placebo effect. The placebo effect, however, can also work in the opposite direction. When researchers gave patients sugar pills but told the patients that they were being given medications that could produce negative side effects, some of the patients developed the side effects, regardless of the fact that they were taking a harmless sugar pill.

of his medication were becoming worse than living with his impulse control disorder. He decided to stop taking lithium and to search for a different treatment option.

Discussion

Everything we put into our bodies has an effect. Most things, we hope, will have a positive effect. Food gives us energy. Water hydrates us. Air provides oxygen to our cells. Unfortunately, other things can have negative effects. Eating peanuts can give energy to one person but can be fatal to a person with a severe peanut allergy. One person may swallow chlorinated water while swimming and feel fine. Another person may swallow the same amount of chlorinated water and feel sick. Medications also have both positive and negative effects. Some people may experience only the positive effects of a given medication. For other people, like Marcus, the negative effects of medication may be so severe that they outweigh any positive gains.

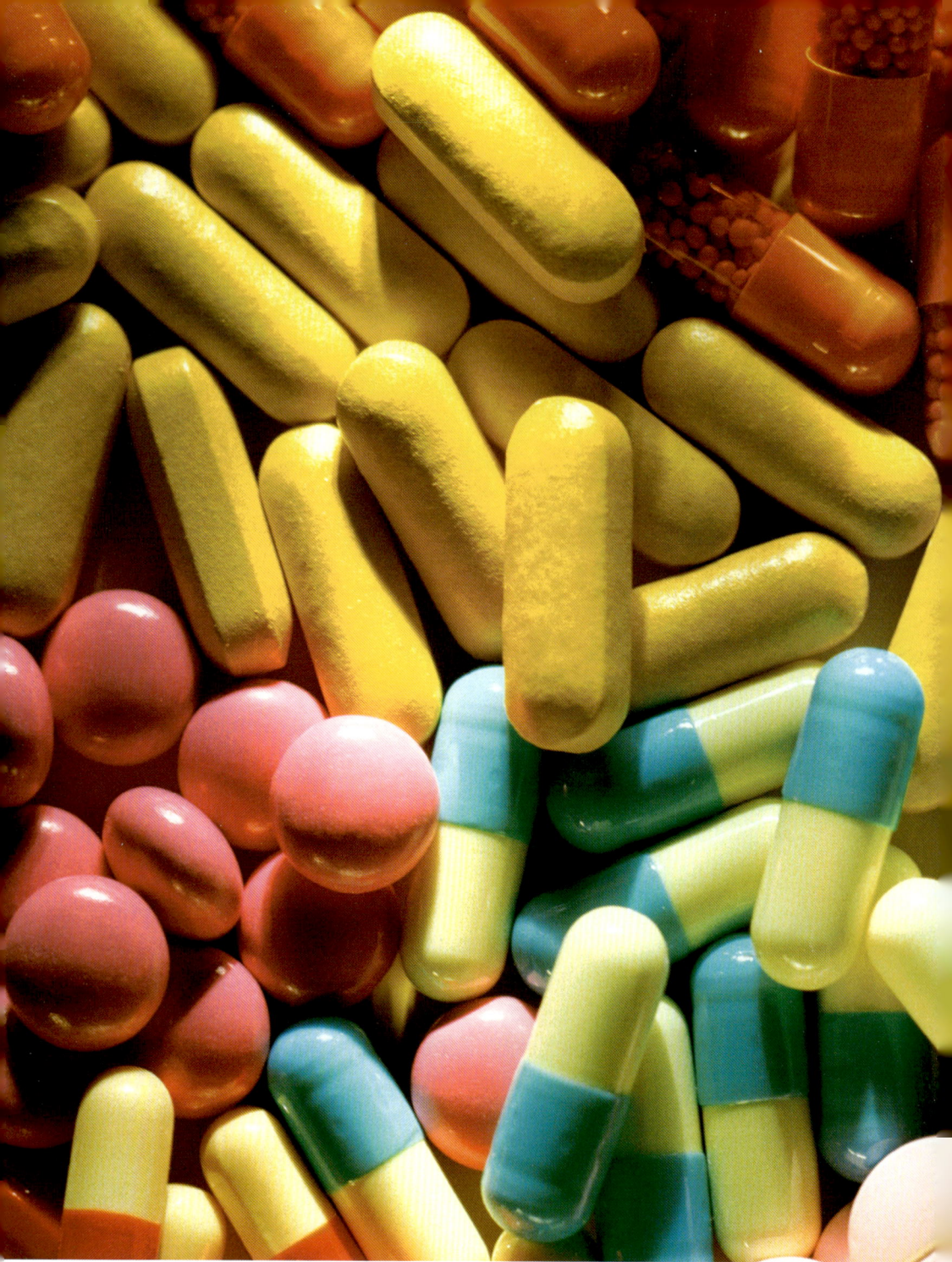

Mixing medications together can be dangerous or even fatal.

Psychiatric drugs have a great range of side effects. They can cause anything from nausea, to sleeplessness, to severe neurological dysfunctions like seizures. Some of the most common side effects of SSRIs and mood stabilizers include somnolence (sleepiness, drowsiness, or fatigue), nausea, diarrhea, and vomiting. Many psychiatric and other types of drugs cannot be mixed with alcohol, aspirin, over-the-counter drugs, or other medications. For some psychiatric medications, something as seemingly simple as having a glass of wine with dinner or taking an over-the-counter cold medication could produce serious, even life-threatening, effects. Patients must be very careful to discuss these issues with a doctor before they begin taking medication.

Women planning to take psychiatric medications should also consider the effects that these drugs might have on fertility and pregnancy. Some psychiatric drugs affect hormone levels in the body, reducing fertility rates. Many psychiatric drugs interact with birth control pills, causing them to lose their effectiveness and increasing the woman's chance of becoming pregnant. This can be very dangerous, because many of these same drugs can also be toxic to the

People who take psychiatric drugs need to carefully balance all factors.

developing fetus. There are cases in which psychiatric drugs have caused conditions such as spina bifida, heart abnormalities, neurological defects, and other birth defects. The vast majority of women taking psychiatric drugs are able to have normal pregnancies and deliver healthy babies, but the benefits and risks of taking medication during pregnancy should always be considered carefully before becoming pregnant. Furthermore, many drugs can be transferred to a baby through the mother's breast milk, so a new mother who is on psychiatric medications may be unable to breastfeed. Many psychiatric medications have not been studied during pregnancy or nursing, so the risks and benefits of drug treatment need to be weighed carefully prior to pregnancy.

spina bifida: A birth defect in which the spinal column has an open area. Sometimes the spinal cord is exposed through the opening in the spinal column.

In some instances side effects may force a person to stop taking medication, but ceasing medication can also be a complicated process. Stopping medication suddenly can produce negative and dangerous side effects of its own. A doctor can counsel a patient on whether her specific medication can be discontinued immediately or if she needs to taper off slowly. The risks and side effects associated with each particular psychiatric drug can be found in *The Physicians' Desk Reference*.

Side effects can happen for many different reasons and do not necessarily mean that a person should stop taking her medication. Some side effects are a sign that the dosage of medication is too high. Lowering the dosage might eliminate the side effects while still providing therapeutic benefits. Other side effects may be temporary, something that the patient feels while her body adjusts to the medication but that will go away with time. Sometimes a patient may even suffer psychosomatic side effects to taking the drug. Side effects like these are caused not by the drug but by the patient's

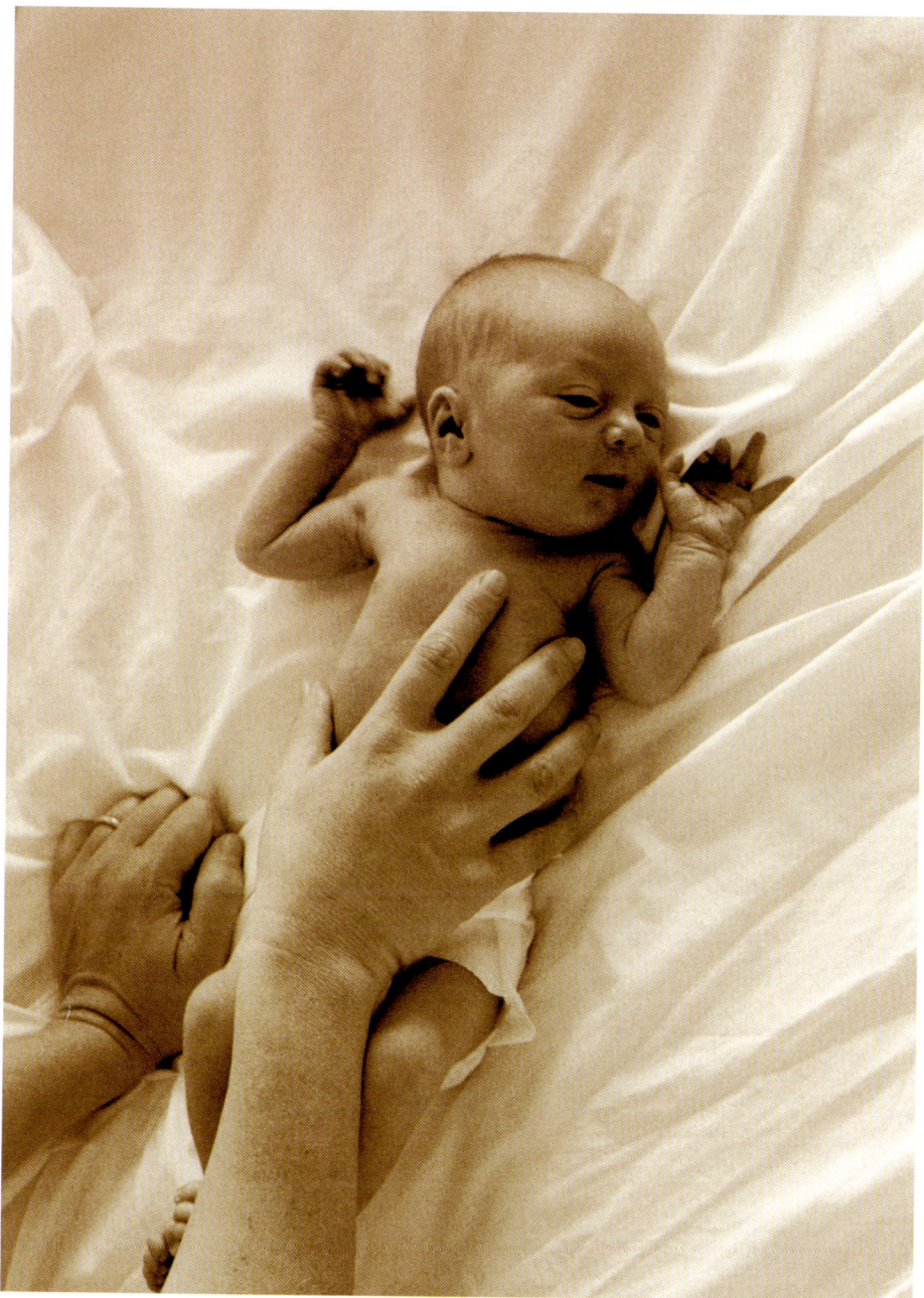

Psychiatric drugs can affect the development of unborn babies, and these chemicals can also be passed to nursing infants through their mothers' milk.

Any side effects a person experiences while taking a psychiatric drug should always be discussed with the prescribing practitioner.

mind. For example, a patient may read a story about a person who became terribly sick when taking a certain medication. When the doctor prescribes this medication for her, she may be so afraid of getting this illness that her brain actually convinces her body that she is sick, even though the drug did not make her ill. Discussing side effects with a doctor can help a patient find out what type of side effects she is having and how best to deal with these effects.

A person who experiences an intermittent explosive disorder may feel isolated and frustrated by his inability to control his emotions.

Chapter Seven

Alternative and Supplementary Treatments

Jerry thought that he would never be cured of his intermittent explosive disorder. In high school, he wasn't even able to play a poker game without freaking out and scaring away his friends. Every time he lost control, he would go back later apologizing and explaining, but he knew nothing he could say would erase what happened.

As time went on, Jerry began pulling away from people to save himself from the hurt and disappointment when his aggression finally drove them away. At the same time, however, he became engrossed in school. He was determined to succeed in life, and he wasn't going to let these explosions stop him. He decided he was going to work hard, go to a great college, and then to medical school.

A person with intermittent explosive disorder may feel as though he has two selves—a "good self" and a dark "bad self."

Group therapy is a major treatment for people with addictions, and as we discussed in chapter two, many people with impulse control disorders experience symptoms similar to those of an addiction. Just as there are groups like Alcoholics Anonymous for people who are addicted to alcohol, there are also groups like Gambler's Anonymous for people who are addicted to gambling.

He was going to become a doctor and find out what was wrong with him and how to fix it. In his last years of high school, this goal became an obsession.

Jerry achieved good grades, a great college record, and entrance to medical school, but at a price. He felt like Jekyl and Hyde, sometimes the nice guy, other times an uncontrollable irrational brute. He would control himself in classes all day, only to finally snap at night. The harder he worked, the more he feared himself. He knew that one of these days it would be the last straw, he would go too far, he would hurt someone, and his professors would find out. When this happened, he knew it would be over. After all, how could he be a doctor if he couldn't control himself around patients?

Jerry was on his psychiatric rotation in medical school when he realized he was never going to make it. Seeing other people with impulse control disorders and how these disorders were affecting their lives made him see he was dealing with his condition all wrong. He was never going to get better if he kept pushing himself, adding more stress, more emotional triggers, more work, and more denial. His schoolwork kept him up until the wee hours of the morning, and his class schedule had him out of bed just a few hours later. When he wasn't trying to control himself during the school day, he was trying to hide from people so they wouldn't find out his secret. Under all this pressure, he knew he would surely snap. Finally, Jerry realized he wasn't going to make it through medical school if he didn't do something about his impulse control disorder. But things had gotten so bad that he wouldn't be able to get help for his impulse control disorder if he didn't change the way he was living. Jerry decided it was time to take a break from school, end his denial, and take control of his life.

When Jerry finally began real treatment for his disorder, he decided to take a holistic approach. He realized that if he wanted to cure his intermittent explosive disorder, he was going to need to address the problems in every area of his life. For five years, Jerry devoted himself to individual and group therapy, anger management courses, yoga classes, exercise, and eating healthy. He forced himself to reconnect with people, making friends, performing community service, joining a synagogue, and anything else that helped him to understand and care for other people. He dedicated himself to learning how to express his emotions, communicate with others, and deal with his anger.

> holistic: Focusing on the whole rather than on parts. Holistic medicine focuses on treating the whole person instead of examining and treating separate parts of the person.

Somewhere in his difficult journey he realized that, even though he had wanted to be a doctor, he loved being with animals. Five years after leaving, Jerry went back to school, this time to become a veterinarian. Jerry felt like his life was finally coming together and that he could look forward to a better future.

Discussion

Like many people with psychiatric disorders, Jerry spent a long time denying his condition. He not only didn't seek proper treatment but he even embarked on a stressful life-style that made his disorder even worse. When he finally did get help for his condition, however, the help came from many sources. The therapy that can improve

The practice of yoga may help with anger management.

Art therapy may provide a constructive outlet for negative emotions.

and cure psychiatric conditions can't happen just inside a therapist's office. It must also extend outside of the office. Jerry realized that he needed to make changes to every part of his life; he needed to supplement his psychiatric therapy in other ways in order to get well.

Despite the fact that medications seem to hold hope for patients with impulse control disorders, such medications are still supplements to the major treatment of psychotherapy. However, medication is not the only way that patients can supplement their therapy. Many people find it helpful to supplement their major therapy with smaller therapeutic elements they can incorporate into their daily lives. For example, doing little things like stopping for a cup of chamomile tea during the day or relaxing in a hot bath with lavender-scented oil after work can do a lot to ease day-to-day stress and tension. Taking yoga and meditation classes can teach people valuable relaxation skills that can be called on in times of stress and crisis. For people with impulse control disorders, a major goal of therapy might be to learn to handle the stresses of everyday life in order to reduce the likelihood of triggering impulsive actions.

Homeopathic Treatment for Impulse Control Disorders

Homeopathy is a form of alternative medicine that treats disease and disorders from a very different perspective from conventional medicine. It looks at a person's entire physical and mental being, rather than dividing a patient into various symptoms and disorders. Homeopathic medicine uses tiny doses to stimulate the body's ability to heal itself. In some cases, these doses may be administered only once every few months or years.

According to Judyth Reichenberg-Ullman and Robert Ullman, authors of *Prozac Free: Homeopathic Medicine for Depression, Anxiety, and Other Mental and Emotional Problems*, homeopathy offers safe, natural alternatives that can supplement or replace conventional pharmaceutical treatment. They recommend this form of treatment because it has fewer side effects than conventional drugs.

In their book, *Anger Kills*, Redford and Virginia Williams give a list of seventeen "Survival Skills" for reducing hostile thoughts, feelings, and actions in your life. They are:
1. Reason with yourself.
2. Stop hostile thoughts, feelings, and urges.
3. Distract yourself.
4. Meditate.
5. Avoid overstimulation.
6. Assert yourself.
7. Care for a pet.
8. Listen.
9. Practice trusting others.
10. Take on community service.

A person with an impulse control disorder may be isolated from the rest of the world, alone in a world of raging emotions. Group therapy may be an effective way to counter these emotions.

11. Increase your empathy.
12. Be tolerant.
13. Forgive.
14. Have a confidant.
15. Laugh at yourself.
16. Become more religious.
17. Pretend today is your last.

Of course, Redford and Virginia Williams are giving suggestions to help people deal with hostile feelings, and these suggestions certainly are not cures for impulse control disorders. In fact, some of these suggestions—such as reason with yourself and stop hostile thoughts, feelings, and urges—might seem almost impossible for a patient with an impulse control disorder. However, making even a few of these adjustments can improve the quality of anybody's life. Even if not providing a cure, improving other aspects of one's life can make facing and dealing with impulse control disorders easier.

Besides making changes like these to one's daily lifestyle, many other supplements to therapy have existed for years with proven benefits. One often important supplement to individual psychotherapy is group therapy. Though most therapists would not recommend group therapy as the primary source of treatment for a person with an impulse control disorder, it can be very helpful as an additional avenue of support. Many patients with impulse control disorders feel alienated from other people. Their illnesses may cause them to feel isolated and to lose friends. In group therapy, patients can meet other people who are experiencing the same difficulties and who understand the hardships of struggling with an impulse control disorder. Patients can find people who sympathize with their experiences. Because the people in group therapy are experiencing the same illness, patients can also be an important resource for each other, sharing information on doctors, treatments, lessons they have learned, and ideas for coping.

As with any treatment, group therapy also has its risks. Some group therapy sessions are run by trained professionals, while others are not. Some people may use group therapy as an outlet for frustration and negative feelings, turning what is meant to be positive into a negative experience. There is also the danger of becoming too reliant on the group therapy and losing the ability to cope outside the support network. As with all treatments, a patient should research carefully before entering into a treatment program.

Impulse control disorders tend to have a great impact on patients' families and friends. For this reason, some patients might want to supplement their individual therapy with family counseling. This is what Donna, whose case was discussed in chapter five, did. She found that family counseling helped her understand how her behavior was affecting those around her. The counseling also helped Donna's parents understand what Donna was going through. Increasing communication and understanding within families in which a person has an impulse control disorder can help everyone involved.

Valerian leaves.

Evening primrose is a natural treatment sometimes used to promote emotional well-being.

"Natural medications" are not approved by the Food and Drug Administration.

As already discussed, medications are also often used as a supplementary treatment both for impulse control disorders and for conditions that may coexist with impulse control disorders. For some people, however, medication is not an option. There are a number of herbal and other natural alternatives that people use for conditions like depression and anxiety—conditions that could make an impulse control disorder more difficult to handle. One of these natural alternatives is Saint-John's-wort.

Saint-John's-wort has been used for many centuries for treating both physical and mental illnesses. This herb has been used in Greece, China, Europe, and North America. Studies in Europe have found Saint-John's-wort to be very effective in treating depression and anxiety, but the United States Food and Drug Administration has not approved it for such treatments. Though it can be purchased over the counter in health food, grocery, and drug stores, one should still do careful research before beginning any medicinal regimen.

Another herb that has been used as a natural remedy for depression and anxiety is kava. Kava is a member of the pepper family and grows in the South Pacific islands. Kava root seems to have a calming effect on the mind. It is also used as a muscle relaxant for the body. In European studies, kava root was said to have the beneficial properties of benzodiazepines (a group of antianxiety medications) without the negative side effects. In very high doses, however, kava may have side effects of its own, including sleepiness and skin irritation. Like Saint-John's-wort, it can be purchased over the counter, but has not been approved for medicinal use by the Food and Drug Administration.

Valerian is yet another herb that has been used for centuries both as a sleep aid and as a temporary remedy for anxiety. It seems to act as a sedative, but as with most herbal remedies, it is not approved by the Food and Drug Administration for medicinal use.

There are many other herbal remedies for conditions like depression and anxiety, but just because a remedy is said to be "natural" doesn't mean that it is safe. Many of our current medications are made from substances that were originally obtained from plants, minerals, and other natural substances. Herbs can have powerful effects on the body and can interact with other medications. You can find more information on herbal remedies at your local library. One should always remember, however, that there are many options a person has before resorting to drugs and complicated herbal remedies. If depression, anxiety, and other difficulties plague you, look at your lifestyle first. Many people are able to obtain relief by making simple but significant changes in the way they live. Do you get a proper amount of sleep? Do you get that sleep at appropriate times (from 10 p.m. to 6 a.m. versus 3 a.m. to 1 p.m.)? Do you eat a healthy diet that is rich in fruits and vegetables and low in fats and sugars? Do you exercise regularly and spend some time outdoors every day? Sometimes, the smallest first steps are the most important ones in changing our lives, and living a healthy lifestyle can make treating an impulse control disorder easier and more effective.

Further Reading

Allen, Thomas E., Mayer C. Liebman, Lee Crandall Park, and William C. Wimmer. *A Primer on Mental Disorders: A Guide for Educators, Families, and Students.* Lanham, Md.: Scarecrow Press, 2001.

Cupchik, Will. *Why Honest People Shoplift or Commit Other Acts of Theft: Assessment and Treatment of "Atypical Theft Offenders."* Toronto, Ont.: Tagami Communications, 2002.

Flannery, Raymond B. *Preventing Youth Violence: A Guide for Parents, Teachers, and Counselors.* New York: Continuum Publishing Group, 1999.

Golomb, Ruth Goldfinger, and Sherrie Mansfield Vavrichek. *The Hair Pulling Habit and You: How to Solve the Trichotillomania Puzzle*. New York: Oxford University Press, 2003.

Shaffer, Howard. *Change Your Gambling, Change Your Life*. San Francisco, Calif.: Jossey-Bass, 2012.

Kolko, David. *Handbook of Firesetting in Children and Youth*. San Diego, Calif.: Academic Press, 2002.

Wambaugh, Joseph. *Fire Lover: A True Story.* New York: HarperCollins, 2002.

Williams, Redford, and Virginia Williams. *Anger Kills: Seventeen Strategies for Controlling the Hostility That Can Harm Your Health.* New York: HarperCollins, 1998.

For More Information

Gamblers Anonymous
www.gamblersanonymous.org

Institute for Brain Aging and Dementia
www.alz.uci.edu

National Institute of Mental Health
www.nimh.nih.gov

The Obsessive Compulsive Foundation, Inc.
www.ocfoundation.org

Psychology Information Online
www.psychologyinfo.com/problems/impulse_control.html

National Association for Shoplifting Prevention
www.shopliftingprevention.org

Trichotillomania Learning Center
www.trich.org

Publisher's Note:
The websites listed on this page were active at the time of publication. The publisher is not responsible for websites that have changed their address or discontinued operation since the date of publication. The publisher will review and update the websites upon each reprint.

Index

About the Author & Consultants

Autumn Libal is a graduate of Smith College and the author of many educational books. She lives and works in Canada.

Mary Ann McDonnell, Ph.D., R.N., is the owner of South Shore Psychiatric Services, where she provides psychiatric services to children and adolescents. She has worked as a psychiatric nurse at Franciscan Hospital for Children and has been a clinical instructor for Northeastern University and Boston College advanced-practice nursing students. She was also the director of clinical trials in the pediatric psychopharmacology research unit at Massachusetts General Hospital. Her areas of expertise are bipolar disorder in children and adolescents, ADHD, and depression.

Donald Esherick has worked in regulatory affairs at Rhone-Poulenc Rorer, Wyeth Pharmaceuticals, Pfizer, and Pharmalink Consulting. He specializes in the chemistry section (manufacture and testing) of investigational and marketed drugs.